John Downes

Roscius Anglicanus

Edited by

Judith Milhous and Robert D. Hume

London

The Society for Theatre Research

1987

First published 1987
by The Society for Theatre Research
Copyright © Judith Milhous and Robert D. Hume
ISBN 0 85430 043 0

Cover and dedication page illustrations are from *Roxburghe Ballads*, ed. William Chappell and J. B. Ebsworth, 9 vols. (Hertford: Printed for the Ballad Society by S. Austin & Sons, 1871-1899). Cover: Woodcut representing Charles II. Dedication page: Woodcut of a fashionable couple from a ballad circa 1685.

Printed at The Bath Press, Avon

For Richard and Janet Macnutt

"The most valuable work of the sort that was ever printed."
John Genest, *Some Account of the English Stage* (1832), I, 27.

"The chronology of John Downes must be regarded as utterly unreliable and uncertain. If this one proviso be kept in mind all other statements in the 'Roscius Anglicanus' may be accepted, unless indeed we have positive evidence to the contrary from strictly contemporary sources of weight and recognized repute."
Montague Summers, Introduction to the edition of 1928

Preface

The importance of *Roscius Anglicanus* to our knowledge of the late seventeenth-century theatre can hardly be overemphasized. Nor, unfortunately, can the dangers of uncritical reliance upon it. Downes is a marvellously pithy source of unique information, but in some respects he is a dangerously unreliable authority. For information about casts, the reception of plays, details of productions, and the success of actors in particular roles, Downes appears quite trustworthy, as far as we can judge from other sources. In matters of chronology he does not: some of his errors are notorious. The organization is minimal, and there are just enough problematical statements in the text to make the work, however valuable, a treacherous prop for the unwary theatre historian.

The first scholarly edition of *Roscius Anglicanus* appeared in 1789, completed by F. G. Waldron, working from notes left by Thomas Davies. Nearly a century later, in 1886, Joseph Knight brought out another, trying to correct some of the factual slips in the Davies-Waldron version and adding anecdotal background. Montague Summers' widely used edition of 1928 was less an attempt to annotate the text than an excuse for long, discursive notes about the actors and plays Downes mentions, an enterprise now rendered largely irrelevant by the Highfill-Burnim-Langhans *Biographical Dictionary*. In recent years most scholars have used the unannotated facsimile of the 1708 edition published in 1969 by the Augustan Reprint Society with an introduction by John Loftis and a useful index by David Stuart Rodes.

The need for a proper modern edition has long been obvious. Our object in editing *Roscius Anglicanus* has been to provide a more readable text than the very chaotic printing job of 1708 and to supply annotation that will guide users safely through the puzzles and errors. We have concentrated on problems of fact, particularly chronology, and have tried to point out Downes' errors, clarify his muddles, and explain his allusions. Our goal has been to help the reader follow Downes without being misled and to supply information (for example, the known dates of actors' activity) that will assist in "applying" Downes.

Prior to the publication of Part 1 of *The London Stage, 1660-1800* in 1965 this edition could not have been done, though there is still a great deal of interesting and important information in *Roscius Anglicanus* not to be found in *The London Stage*. Likewise, the availability of the *Biographical Dictionary* is a godsend to the editor of Downes, and we are grateful to the authors for their generous permission to make use of their files on those performers who fall in volumes yet unpublished.

Some of Downes' tangles will probably always remain insoluble, but given the advances in modern scholarship on which we have been able to draw, a surprising number can be sorted out. Some treacherous shoals remain, but we have tried to mark them clearly enough that future scholars will be able to use *Roscius Anglicanus* with greater confidence than has hitherto been possible.

JM & RDH

The University of Maryland
The Pennsylvania State University
September 1986

Contents

Introduction

In 1708 *Roscius Anglicanus* was an enterprise virtually without model or precedent in England. We have no way to guess where Downes got the idea or what served as his inspiration in design and method. Nor do we know what documentary materials he had available. That the results are disjointed and sometimes inaccurate—not to mention infuriatingly selective—cannot be denied. But if we consider the state of literary history at the start of the eighteenth century, we must acknowledge that what Downes managed to write is a surprising and impressively specific achievement.

As of 1708 no one in England had written anything that could legitimately be described as "an historical review" of literature or drama.[1] Gerard Langbaine's *An Account of the English Dramatick Poets* (1691) is basically a list of published plays organized by author. We should not denigrate Langbaine: he was a formidably thorough bibliographer; his attention to attribution problems is remarkably careful; his concern for identification of adaptations and sources is decades ahead of his time. Langbaine's comments show that he attended the theatre, but his aim was to provide a catalogue of printed plays. He mentions success in performance only in occasional asides, and his discussions of authors rarely go beyond an attempt to identify them. Biographical attention to playwrights was in its infancy; biographical interest in actors could hardly be said to exist. The first life of an English actor was Tobyas Thomas' *The Life of the Late Famous Comedian, Jo Hayns* (1701), a scandal pamphlet concocted by a minor actor to exploit interest in Haines' chequered career at the time of his death. Thomas' concern is with name-dropping and racy anecdotes, not with Haines as an actor. Even Charles Gildon's *The Life of Mr. Thomas Betterton* (1710) contains no more than a few scrappy bits of biographical information.

---

[1] See René Wellek, *The Rise of English Literary History* (Chapel Hill: Univ. of North Carolina Press, 1941).

Most of the text consists of Gildon's treatise on the art of acting—much of it plagiarized from French elocution books, adapted crudely to the context of the English theatre, and stuffed into "Betterton's" mouth. But Gildon appears after Downes: we cite the *Life* as an example of the minimal state of history and biography as they related to the stage around this time. Only one work before Downes shows even the rudiments of a "historical" approach to the English theatre—James Wright's *Historia Histrionica* (1699). Wright's little pamphlet is a peculiar amalgam, combining scattered comments on actors' roles and training before 1642 with a sketchy general parallel between the history of drama in Greece and its development in England. *Historia Histrionica* provides some useful scraps of information, but it is essentially the gleanings and speculations of a dilettante, and it offered nothing like a model for Downes.

What we know of John Downes himself is close to nil. By his own account he was "spoil'd . . . for an Actor" by the sight of the King and the Duke of York at the première of Part 1 of *The Siege of Rhodes* (p. 73),[2] an admission confirmed by Pepys' comment on 2 July that the Eunuch was so much out in his lines that he was hissed off the stage. What Downes' background and age were, whether he attempted other parts, when he became prompter—of such matters we know nothing. His name appears occasionally in the Lord Chamberlain's records. He was sworn as a comedian "to attend his Royall Highnesse the Duke of Yorke" on 27 June 1664, and was sworn as a King's comedian 12 January 1687[/8], again on 22 February 1694/5, and a third time ca. 20 April 1697.[3] James Gowslaw asked permission to sue him on 3 April 1665, as did Richard Skayfe on 26 June 1667.[4] After that Downes evidently paid his bills, for we have no further record of requests to sue him.

The probability seems to be that Downes joined the house staff at Lincoln's Inn Fields soon after his fiasco in *The Siege of Rhodes*

---

[2] An event that occurred in June 1661 at the opening of the Lincoln's Inn Fields theatre.

[3] P.R.O. LC 3/25, p. 162; LC 3/30, p. 113; LC 3/31, p. 108; LC 3/3, fol. 25.

[4] LC 5/186, fols. 58v, 151.

and became prompter sometime in the next few years. By his own statement he "continu'd" as "Book-keeper and Prompter . . . till *October 1706*" (p. 2); we infer that he was forced into retirement at the time of the proto-union of 1706. Whether Downes wrote *Roscius Anglicanus* to occupy himself in retirement or to try to make a bit of money we do not know, but if the latter, he was probably disappointed. The book appears to have sunk without trace upon publication, and from the scarcity of extant copies today we would deduce a meagre sale. Luttrell's copy (now in the hands of a private collector) is annotated "20 July" (written beside "1708" on the title page) and "4ᵈ." Downes probably did need money. Some three months after the reorganization of 1706, Owen Swiney—then managing the Haymarket company—wrote to the Lord Chamberlain to explain that "young Downes" had not been hired as a musician because he was unqualified, but that the theatre would give Downes' father whatever pension the Lord Chamberlain thought fit.[5] A letter written in response to the *Tatler* of 22 September 1709 comments that "Mr. *Downs*, who had been prime Minister to so many Buskin'd Monarchs, is thrown aside into a Pension, which, like those at Court, are not long well paid."[6] We have no evidence that Downes ever returned to an active job in the theatre. A letter in the *Tatler* of 1 July 1710 purports to be from Downes. It says that Christopher Rich has offered him a job as prompter for a scratch company (which never materialized) at Drury Lane. The chances are that Steele was merely making use of Downes' name, for the point of the letter is to mock Rich. The old prompter may have died in 1712: *The Registers of St. Paul's Church, Covent Garden, London* record the burial of a John Downes on 4 June 1712.[7]

---

[5] LC 7/3, fols. 94-95 (letter of 27 January 1706[/7]).

[6] First published in *The Post-Man Robb'd of his Mail* [ed. Charles Gildon] (London: Bettesworth and Rivington, 1719), p. 266. The authors of the *Biographical Dictionary* took this as evidence that Downes was still alive in 1719, but Bruce Podewell has pointed out that internal evidence places the letter ca. October 1709. See "New Light on John Downes," *Notes and Queries*, 223 (1978), 24.

[7] Publications of the Harleian Society, Registers, vol. 36 (London, 1908), St. Paul's, Covent Garden, IV, 226. This record was first noted by

For personal commentary on Downes we have only one source, and that an extremely hostile one. The anonymous author of *The Players turn'd Academicks* (1703), a derisive account of the Lincoln's Inn Fields company's visit to Oxford in July 1703, devoted some twenty lines to the old prompter.[8]

> *Jack D—n*'s was resolv'd to make one with the Rest,
> And amongst 'em he thrust in his Corps, and his Jest,
> Both useless and old, and as much out of Date,
> As his Notional Form of a Common-wealth State,
> Which he had been hammering out of his Poll,
> And pleasing Old *Nickby*, in commending Old *Noll*.
>
> The Republican Dotard sate stinking and sweating,
> And tagging his Lies with the Points of false Latin,
> While he set abroach Schemes, could be ne're put in Practice,
> And attested with Oaths what no Matter of Fact is,
> As he gave strange Accounts both of Farces and Plays,
> And brag'd of things done, in *Hart*'s and *Mohun*'s Days.
>
> The Company smoak'd what he meant by his Prating,
> And excus'd him from paying for Drinking and Eating,
> By letting him Spunge both for Victuals and Bub,
> And lay down his impudent Lies for his Club;
> For he durst not for fear of great hazard of Life,
> But bring what he Got to his Termagant Wife,
> Who had Midwif'd him out of his *Money* and *Wit*,
> And prompted the *Prompter* to do what she thought fit,
> As she Reign'd him, and Rid him, with Spur and with Bit.

About all we learn from this is that Downes had some pretensions to a classical education, which suggests that his epigraph and Latinisms (e.g., "Aspectabund," p. 108) are his own proud doing.

John Loftis in his introduction to the 1969 Augustan Reprint Society edition, p. iv.

[8] *The Players turn'd Academicks* (London, 1703), p. 7. British Library 11795.k.31 (2). Arnott and Robinson, no. 1671.

In writing *Roscius Anglicanus* Downes' greatest advantage was that he could work from personal knowledge. "I relate not hearsay, but experience," as his epigraph informs us. What sources of information he was able to draw on, other than memory, we do not know. Summers expresses long-standing opinion when he says that "it would appear that in his narrative he was trusting largely to memory, and that he had at hand few, if any, actual manuscript notes by which to check his chronicle" (1928 edition, p. vii). In matters of dates and chronology this view is hard to quarrel with: if Downes had been working from any sort of diary or official records he could scarcely have arrived at so jumbled an order for the plays. Casts are a completely different matter. Had Downes been relying on memory for early casts (e.g., *Cutter of Coleman-Street*, 1661, p. 57) numerous slips, contradictions, and impossibilities would almost certainly have come to light. Downes' dubious reputation notwithstanding, we must emphasize that nearly two hundred years of skeptical scrutiny by scholars expecting the worst have produced only a tiny handful of queries about his casts—most of them concerning the King's Company and (as we shall see) most of them without foundation.

Downes might well have been able to use the records of the company at the theatre in the Haymarket in 1707 while he was writing his history, but those records—if any, and whatever they may have consisted of—would probably have gone no further back than 1695, when that company was founded. Marked prompt copies from the Duke's and United Company years presumably stayed at Drury Lane in 1695, and Christopher Rich does not seem likely to have allowed Downes access to such records as Drury Lane held in 1707. Certainly such access cannot be demonstrated from the text of *Roscius Anglicanus*. Downes may have kept notes of his own. We might hypothesize that he wrote casts (but not dates of performance) in personal copies of plays, which would account for some of the anomalies in *Roscius Anglicanus*; but this is pure speculation.

We must admire Downes' determination to cover the King's Company. All we know about how he obtained his information is his own terse and ungrammatical explanation: "But as to the Actors of *Drury-Lane* Company, under Mr. *Thomas Killigrew*, he having the Account from Mr. *Charles Booth* sometimes Book-keeper there" (p. 2). Unfortunately, we know nothing else of Booth. Was

he Downes' counterpart with the rival company in the sixties? Did
he join in the 1670s? When did Downes obtain the King's Company
casts he prints—at the time of the amalgamation of the two companies in 1682, or when he was actually writing *Roscius Anglicanus* in
1707? That Downes could name minor and temporary King's Company personnel of circa 1660 from memory some forty-five years
later seems highly unlikely. The chances are good that Downes
simply took over his King's Company information from Booth. But
what did Booth work from? Not from play quartos (there are no
quarto casts for many of the plays); conceivably from memory; conceivably from records in the possession of the Killigrew family.

However Downes obtained his material, he did little to give it
any semblance of structure and organization. Because he uses no
subheadings of any sort, his narrative seems a good deal more chaotic than it actually is. An editor might break it up as follows:

Part I: The King's Company
   1. The Establishment of the Company (pp. 3-9)
   2. Old Stock Plays (pp. 10-25)
   3. New Stock Plays (pp. 25-40)
   4. Summary Overview of the Company (pp. 40-42)

Part II: The Duke's Company
   1. The Establishment of the Company (pp. 42-50)
   2. Plays 1661-1665 (pp. 50-59)
   3. Plays 1666-1671 (pp. 59-68)
   4. Plays at Dorset Garden 1671-1674 and
      Roster Changes (pp. 68-75)
   5. Plays 1675-1682 (pp. 75-81)

Part III: The United Company
   1. The Union of 1682 (pp. 81-82)
   2. Plays 1682-1694 (pp. 82-90)

Part IV: The Lincoln's Inn Fields Company and Beyond
   1. The Actor Rebellion and the New Company
      (pp. 91-92)

So viewed, *Roscius Anglicanus* is quite tidily laid out. Inevitably,
there is chronological repetition in the first two parts, but thereafter
Downes follows a single, linear progression. Yet somehow every-
thing runs together in his recital: there are no highlightings, summaries, and transitions of the sort that place a historian's subject in
perspective. Downes reports changes in management and owner-
ship such as the Union of 1682 and the actor rebellion of 1694-95,
but in a curiously flat and neutral way. His interest lies in plays
and performers, not in management.

Downes' focus and particular slant clearly derive from his
many years as prompter. His outlook is unabashedly commercial:
"twas very Gainful to the Company" (p. 89); "The Court and Town
were wonderfully satisfy'd with it; but the Expences in setting it out
being so great, the Company got very little by it" (p. 89); "got the
Company Money" (p. 93); "answer'd not the Expences they were
at in Cloathing it" (p. 94). Almost every page of narrative has such
a comment. Mention of the literary or dramaturgical quality of
plays is almost always secondary to other considerations: Did it
"take"? Was there something special about the production? That a
play succeeded, or failed, or provided a good vehicle for Elizabeth
Barry, or was mounted with new scenery and costumes—these are
matters far more important to Downes than what year the play
was first produced or whether it came before or after another one.
What he wrote is more like "annals" than "history properly so
called" (to borrow a distinction from Dryden), but though his organization is ostensibly chronological, his concern is not with chronology.
Downes rarely tries to assign plays to particular years; the drama
historian's mania for studying new plays in chronological order is a
concept alien to the prompter's outlook. Downes' priorities are in
fact clearly signalled on the title page. He gives "The Names of the
Principal Actors and Actresses, who Perform'd in the Chiefest Plays
in each House. With the Names of the most taking Plays; and Modern Poets." When Downes says "the next new Play . . .," we must
realize that this is a conventional formula, not a literal specification

of fact. He probably had no way to determine the order in which new plays received their premières in, say, 1674, and we see no signs that he cared.

Downes' simple errors in dates are less distressing than his pretense of chronological order within each section. When he says that the Bridges Street theatre opened on 8 April 1663, or that *Cambyses* was the first new play performed in 1666 after the reopening of the theatres, or that *Psyche* received its première in February 1673, he is simply wrong, and we can correct the error. But when Downes presents a list of plays ostensibly in order of production (as, for example, on pages 75-80), and we discover that it has only the vaguest resemblance to the sequence we can verify, we have reason to feel that Downes is misleading. Within his subgroupings the order of the plays is often little better than random.

Early twentieth-century scholars tended either to follow Downes blithely into error or to fling up their hands in disgust. W. J. Lawrence describes *Roscius Anglicanus* as "A rambling stage record published in 1708, when the quondam prompter who penned it was in the decline of his years and intellect. . . . It cannot be too strongly emphasized that through slovenliness of arrangement the 'Roscius Anglicanus' is positively honeycombed with error. . . . It is the old story of a senile memory with nothing to check its vagaries."[9] Harsh as it is, this view is understandable: if chronology is our touchstone, then *Roscius Anglicanus* is worse than worthless. If, however, we can accept the fact that chronology was of little or no interest to Downes, then we can usefully enquire how well his assertions about casts, attributions, and popularity stand up under close examination. The answer is that those that can be checked stand up astonishingly well.

This may seem a surprising assertion, since in recent years Downes has been condemned for providing "composite" casts—an attitude evident in the way his casts have been handled in *The London Stage* and the *Biographical Dictionary*. The charge now appears unjust. It has stemmed almost entirely from his King's Company casts for *Rule a Wife*, *The Maid's Tragedy*, and *The Elder Brother*

---

[9] W. J. Lawrence, *The Elizabethan Playhouse and Other Studies* (Stratford-upon-Avon: Shakespeare Head Press, 1912), pp. 214-215.

(pp. 11-12, 15-16, 18-19), which include "Mrs. Boutel." Since Elizabeth Bowtell does not otherwise appear in the records until 1670, and Walter Clun (who is also listed in *Rule a Wife*) died in August 1664, scholars have concluded that Downes—perhaps more fairly we should say Charles Booth—pieced together these casts from memory, conflating productions from different decades in the process. But this is not the case, for the damning evidence of Mrs. Bowtell turns out to be no evidence at all. Bowtell is the married name of Elizabeth Davenport, who was with the company in 1667 and could perfectly well have joined in 1664 or earlier.[10] This discovery goes a long way toward exonerating Downes from the worst charges of incompetence.

To assess Downes' casts fairly, we must reject two false assumptions about them. Both concern the casts for the King's Company's "Principal Old Stock Plays" (pp. 10-24). The first is that the casts represent—or are supposed to represent—the earliest Restoration performances of the plays at issue. This notion is evident in the desire of the *London Stage* editors to assign each cast to the earliest documented performance date. The case of *A King and no King* illustrates the dangers of this approach: the play was definitely in the company's repertory in 1660-61, but Nell Gwyn, whom Downes includes, seems not to have joined the company until circa 1663-64. The second false assumption is that these casts are specifically associated with the Bridges Street theatre. Downes' placement of the cast lists after his account of the opening of the new theatre seems at first glance to imply that they originated there (p. 9). But analysis of the very first cast warns us to beware of such tidy divisions. Downes names Clun as the title character in *The Humorous Lieutenant*; yet we know from Pepys (8 May 1663) that Lacy replaced Clun as the Lieutenant in the Bridges Street production at the command of the King. Hence Downes' cast is presumably for earlier performances at Vere Street. What Downes is treating in this section is old stock plays belonging to the King's Company, not plays (or productions) new to this theatre.

Having studied the twenty-nine King's Company casts in

---

[10] See Judith Milhous, "Elizabeth Bowtell and Elizabeth Davenport: Some Puzzles Solved," *Theatre Notebook*, 39 (1985), 124-134.

Roscius Anglicanus, we have concluded that there is no reason to challenge the legitimacy of any of them. By this we mean that there is no instance in which we can show that any of the casts could not have been assembled at *some* time. There is, however, no easy way to categorize them. For new plays the casts are almost always from the first production—but evidently not in the case of *Sophonisba*. For many revivals the lists represent neither the earliest known performance nor the latest; why *these* casts are given is impossible to say. The temptation to associate Downes' casts for revivals with known performance dates, as the editors of *The London Stage* endeavoured to do, is misguided. Because our records are extremely scanty, lack of a known performance date at a time when all of Downes' performers would have been available proves nothing about the validity of his casts. There is no reason why a given cast of his should match a performance just because we happen to have a record of one. Methodologically, the only sound procedure is to assume that the cast is correct for *some* period of time, and to attempt to deduce the span of months or years over which the named performers could have been assembled. In some cases this is a long period, in others a very short one. Downes' cast for *The Silent Woman* would evidently have been available from the autumn of 1664 (when Knepp joined the company) to 1677 (when Rutter left). By way of contrast, Downes' cast for *The Rival Queens* pertains only to the original production of March 1677, since Rebecca Marshall left the company the next month.[11]

---

[11] Arthur H. Scouten argues at length that "the majority" of the first series of King's Company casts pertain to performances "after the hiatus of the plague and fire of 1665-66." See "A Reconsideration of the King's Company Casts in John Downes' *Roscius Anglicanus*," *Theatre Notebook*, 40 (1986), 74-85. (We are grateful to Professor Scouten for making a copy of his article available to us in proof.) We agree that very few of the casts could date from as early as 1661, but we are not convinced by Scouten's attempt to associate Downes' casts with particular performance dates. The performance records are so sketchy that any association of cast and date becomes extremely arbitrary. And Scouten arrives at some of his dates for casts in odd ways. For example, he ignores evidence that Mrs. Rutter was sworn as a member of the company in 1661, and he insists

Far fewer questions have been raised about the Duke's Company casts, largely because they are almost always for new productions and hence comparatively easy to date. One of the principal challenges concerns the cast for Etherege's *The Man of Mode* (March 1676), in which Downes names Elizabeth Barry as Mrs. Loveit. We must agree that this is a surprising role for an inexperienced actress, but a careful investigation of all the evidence does not substantiate John Harold Wilson's conjecture (accepted by the *London Stage* editors) that the role originally belonged to Mary Lee and that Barry took it over circa 1685.[12] In all probability, Downes was right.

For the theatre historian, Downes' casts are the most vital part of his book, and they withstand scrutiny surprisingly well. What can be checked almost always proves correct. One measure of the accuracy of Downes' casts is their high degree of conformity with the casts printed in quartos. His casts are rarely as full as those in the quartos—he usually names only the principals—but the agreement is striking. Of course, Downes may have gone to the printed plays for some of his casts, or corrected from them, but if so he consistently edited out minor characters. And quite a few of his casts *must* come from somewhere else, since the relevant quartos contain no cast at all. Downes is our only source for a large number of Duke's Company casts, especially in the first fifteen years of the period, and assurance of their probable reliability is welcome indeed.

Downes is no miracle of accuracy (even in non-dating matters), and *Roscius Anglicanus* should certainly not be read uncritically. A footnote to point out that *"St. James's-Park"* is merely an alternative title for *Love in a Wood* in the same list (p. 40) does not come

---

(implausibly, in our view) that Lacy replaced Clun in the title role of *The Humorous Lieutenant* on the King's orders with less than twenty-four hours' notice on 8 May 1663. Attractive as Scouten's theories of origin and assignment may be, we continue to believe that the only sound methodology is to present the span of dates over which each of Downes' casts would have been available. Eleven of the fifteen casts at issue *could* have been assembled before the closing of the theatres in June 1665.

[12] See Robert D. Hume, "Elizabeth Barry's First Roles and the Cast of *The Man of Mode*," *Theatre History Studies*, 5 (1985), 16-19.

amiss, nor does a caution against Downes' misleading comment on
"*Two Fools well met*, by Mr. *Lodwick Carlile*" (p. 67). Readers must
beware of Downes' quirks. He is quite inconsistent, for example,
about informing the reader that Mary Saunderson became Mrs.
Betterton; Mary Aldridge became Mrs. Lee and later Lady
Slingsby; Elizabeth Davenport became Mrs. Bowtell; Anne Gibbs
married Thomas Shadwell. In this respect he is not wrong, but he
is often unhelpful. The dangers of taking "the next new play" literally have already been noted. Another such problem is posed by
Downes' habit of specifying the length of unusually successful first
runs. Interpreting these figures is difficult. For example, he claims
that Shadwell's *The Sullen Lovers* (May 1668) was "Acted 12 Days
together"(p. 64)—a quite extraordinary initial run in this period.
However, *The London Stage* shows that, given the Duke's Company's known offerings, there is no two-week span in which Shadwell's play *could* have enjoyed an unbroken run of twelve days. It
was undoubtedly very popular, and it may well have received a
dozen performances in short order, but "12 Days together" is not
literally true.

    Roscius Anglicanus is an old man's book, and if one grants the
inaccuracy of its chronology, it is a more trustworthy document
than we have any right to expect. What Downes cares about he
tends to get right. Too much has been made of his blunders, most
of which are easily spotted and corrected. The discoveries of recent
scholars enable us to use him with reasonable confidence. Though
there are pitfalls to be avoided—and charting the user's way
through them is the principal object of this edition—we should not
underestimate the degree to which Downes can be relied upon. An
intensive review of the facts in *Roscius Anglicanus*, conducted with
all the advantages of modern scholarship at our disposal, leads us to
reaffirm Montague Summers' view of the work: to trust Downes in
anything connected with dates or chronological order is madness,
but on other matters his word can be accepted unless we have particular reason to doubt it. This is a welcome conclusion. Emmett L.
Avery, a scholar whose work we much admire, was so dubious
about Downes' reliability that when he compiled Part 2 of *The London Stage* he ignored virtually all of Downes' many comments on
casts and the success of plays between 1700 and 1706. In retro-
spect, this seems an excess of caution. *Roscius Anglicanus* is rich in
firsthand information, much of it unique and exceedingly valuable to

the theatre historian. A judicious skepticism is seldom amiss, but (chronology always excepted) we have more reason to trust Downes than to doubt him.

Roscius Anglicanus is a wonderfully terse and trenchant book, not only a pleasure to read and a rich source of theatre history, but a fascinating expression of its author's outlook. Downes is engagingly free of pretension and theory; he simply tells us what plays the companies he worked for staged, how well they succeeded, and who performed in them. The resulting book is as valuable as it is anomalous.

Editorial Policy

The text

We have adopted an unusual layout. We wanted to put as many of the notes as possible at the foot of the appropriate page— but also to record the 1708 pagination in some way so that scholars would not have to turn elsewhere to follow up references in the many books and articles that refer to the original, to Summers' pseudo facsimile, or to the Augustan Reprint Society facsimile. Consequently we have put all but the longest notes at the foot of the page while indicating the original 1708 page numbers in brackets in the text—[7] and so forth. Thus while this edition has its own page numbers, and a full index keyed to that pagination, users will be able to locate passages from references to the original edition or facsimiles of it.

Downes' text presents the editor with exceptional difficulties. His idiosyncratic syntax and his bizarre capitalization, italics, and punctuation, make normal old-spelling policy almost beside the point. One can see why Knight and Summers opted for pseudo facsimile. Waldron, who did some regularization and correction, asks "indulgence for whatever may appear amiss in this edition; the original is in many respects so faulty, that to have endeavoured to amend it in any material degree, would have been to re-write, not

re-print it."[13] To modernize is to lose Downes' tone and flavour, as
well as to risk distorting his meanings. To reprint the text verbatim
is unhelpful, littered as it is with errors and irregularities of every
sort.

Our solution is frankly unorthodox. We present an old-spelling
text, but with rather freer amendments than are customary in such
editions. We have left Downes' odd syntax as is, but we have
reduced eccentric mid-word capitals to lower case (while leaving the
majority of Downes' capitals as Henry Playford originally printed
them), and we have converted some italic capitals to roman. Thus
"THE first Compos'd by *Mr. Lock*" becomes "The first Compos'd by
Mr. *Lock*" (p. 71). We have allowed most of the italics to stand, but
have reduced them to roman where the original is confusing, especially when titles are run into the text. Thus "in this Play *Mr.
Jevon Acting* a *Chinese* Prince" becomes "in this Play Mr. *Jevon*
Acting a *Chinese* Prince" (p. 75), and *"The Soldiers Fortune, Wrote
by Mr.* Otway" becomes *"The Soldiers Fortune*, Wrote by Mr.
Otway" (p. 77). In the latter case our logic is that we should disen-
tangle the title, while preserving the emphasis on the author's name
conferred by typographical difference; Playford almost always sets
names in italics, unless he is trying to distinguish them from italics.
Play titles originally set in roman or a mixture of roman and italics
have been silently converted to italics. In a number of passages we
have silently reversed italics and roman, on the assumption that
although we should preserve the book's usual typographical distinc-
tions there is no reason slavishly to follow the eccentricities of Playford's printing job. Single words, especially verbs, set in italics for
no visible reason have been silently converted to roman. Long S is,
of course, not reproduced here. Reversed type is corrected silently,
except when a possible word or a name is emended. Since
Downes—or Playford—normally puts a period after "Mr." and
"Mrs.," we have silently inserted periods in a few places where they
are missing. Likewise we have silently altered occasional periods to
commas after names of characters in conformity with Downes'
usual practice in tabular cast lists. Abbreviations evidently imposed
by the printer for reasons of space—e.g., "Q." for "Queen"—have

---

[13] Waldron (1789), facing p. 70.

been expanded and the change recorded in the Textual Notes. A particular format problem is posed by the printer's placement of explanatory comments in small boxes within the text. Modern printing processes do not readily allow for this practice, but to print such passages as footnotes (even labelled as "Downes' note") would bury them in our own voluminous notes. In four instances we have dealt with this problem by running Downes' boxed comments into the text as separate paragraphs at a logical point, calling attention to the fact in a footnote (original pages 25, 27, 40, 41). We have seen no reason to preserve silly errors—for example, the misnumbering of plays on pages 17-22 or "Mr. Knep" on page 22. All such corrections are recorded in the Textual Notes.

Our copytext is the Newberry copy. It has been collated against the Folger, Johns Hopkins (Peabody Collection), Harvard, Texas (truncated at page 34), and British Library copies (C.27.d.14. and C.31.h.41), as well as the Augustan Reprint Society facsimile (a composite of the Folger and Huntington copies) and two copies in the possession of a private collector who prefers to remain anonymous. All departures from copytext not covered in this statement of textual policy are recorded in the textual notes with the exception of punctuation that failed to ink properly. The careless presswork in Playford's edition led to a fair number of cases in which letters did not print clearly, and some punctuation may be faint or invisible in any one copy. Our policy has been to print such a character (especially commas, periods, hyphens, and apostrophes) without a textual note if we found it clearly visible in any one of the ten copies we collated. Where we have added punctuation on our own authority, we have invariably recorded the emendation in the textual notes. The eight errata on A1v of the Playford edition have been duly incorporated in the text, though we agree with Joseph Knight that "*Page* 2, *Read* Reeves, *for* Knight" should read "*Page* 3 . . ." and have handled the affected portion of the text accordingly. Since all departures from copytext are editorial, we have not distinguished what we regard as "corrections" from "emendations" in the textual notes.

One textual red-herring needs to be noted and dismissed. In the introduction to his edition Montague Summers states that "there were various issues [of *Roscius Anglicanus* in 1708], and in certain of these the author corrected some few of the more patent errors due to the printer's carelessness or haste" (p. x). Although

Summers did not introduce any alternative readings from these alleged variant issues into his text or notes, his assertion has been quoted by Arnott and Robinson in their entry for *Roscius Anglicanus* (A&R, no. 824). We have, however, discovered no copies exhibiting variant states of the text, and we doubt that any exist. We would guess that Summers got this idea from volume 2 of Richard John Smith's "A Collection of Material towards an History of the English Stage," preserved in the British Library (shelfmark 11826 r,s), where there is a copy of the 1789 edition heavily marked with "variants" and a note by "J. Broughton": "There must have been two Editions of this Book [i.e., the Playford edition of 1708], or (which is more probable) he made alterations in some of the sheets, as it passed through the Press: I have a Copy presenting many variations from the text of that which appears to have been used for this reprint. The most remarkable of them I have noted in the margin." What Broughton has in fact marked appear to be errors in the 1789 edition, which is by no means the accurate reprint of 1708 it claims to be. We cannot prove that this is the source of Summers' airy assertion about variant states, but it seems a likely possibility. We have found no press corrections in the 1708 edition.

Annotation

Our aim has been to supply such facts as the reader may need to comprehend *Roscius Anglicanus* and to use it without fear of being misled by Downes' muddles and mistakes. We have drawn freely on the notes of Davies, Waldron, Knight, and Summers (indicating the source in each instance), but we have not felt obliged to correct their erroneous annotation (except in a few special instances) or to repeat, even in summary form, their many inflated and tangentially relevant notes. Our concern has been with corrections and identifications, not with the context and background material needed to appreciate or apply Downes fully. When facts can readily be verified by reference to a name in the *Biographical Dictionary* or a date in *The London Stage*, we have usually just given the fact (for example, that Nicholas Blagden worked briefly for the Duke's Company but switched to the King's Company by December 1661). When facts can be verified only from less obvious published sources, or from unpublished material, we have given full documentation.

A note on dates and titles

Most playdates and performance records are drawn from *The London Stage*. When dates vary from what is given there, the difference will be explained in the new editions of Parts 1 and 2 on which we are at work. For a significant number of these cases the reader may consult our article, "Dating Play Premières from Publication Data, 1660-1700," *Harvard Library Bulletin*, 22 (1974), 374-405. Dates of pre-1660 plays are normally taken from Alfred Harbage, *Annals of English Drama, 975-1700*, rev. S. Schoenbaum (London: Methuen, 1964). Users of this edition should note that all dates are Old Style and that the new year is treated as beginning on 1 January rather than on 25 March. When we quote dates employing (or possibly employing) the old year-change convention, we have so indicated with brackets—e.g., 20 February 1667[/8] or 20 February 1667[/8?].

In all cases we have left Downes' eccentric forms of play titles uncorrected in the text. Thus *Volpone* appears as *The Fox* (with a cross-reference in the index), and *Aureng-Zebe* appears as *Aureng Zeb*. In our notes and in the index, however, we have almost always used standard forms and spellings of the titles—even though this means that *Cataline* and *Catiline* may appear on the same page.

Acknowledgements

For assistance of various sorts we are grateful to William J. Burling, John Brett-Smith, Wilma R. Ebbitt, John T. Harwood, Kathryn Hume, Charles W. Mann, Jr., and George Speaight. We want to express our special appreciation to Thomas Minsker for generous help with computer formatting and printing.

Works Frequently Cited and Abbreviations

Apology——*An Apology for the Life of Mr. Colley Cibber, Comedian*, ed. Robert W. Lowe, 2 vols. (1889; rpt. New York: AMS Press, 1966).

Arnott and Robinson——*English Theatrical Literature 1559-1900: A Bibliography*, comp. James Fullarton Arnott and John William Robinson (London: Society for Theatre Research, 1970).

"Attribution Problems"——Judith Milhous and Robert D. Hume, "Attribution Problems in English Drama, 1660-1700," *Harvard Library Bulletin*, 31 (1983), 5-39.

Bentley——Gerald Eades Bentley, *The Jacobean and Caroline Stage*, 7 vols. (Oxford: Clarendon Press, 1941-1968).

Biographical Dictionary——Philip H. Highfill, Jr., Kalman A. Burnim, and Edward A. Langhans, *A Biographical Dictionary of Actors, Actresses, Musicians, Dancers, Managers & Other Stage Personnel in London, 1660-1800*, 18 vols. in progress (Carbondale: Southern Illinois Univ. Press, 1973—).

A Comparison Between the Two Stages——Anon., *A Comparison Between the Two Stages* (1702), ed. Staring B. Wells (Princeton: Princeton Univ. Press, 1942).

Congreve: Letters and Documents——*William Congreve: Letters and Documents*, ed. John C. Hodges (New York: Harcourt, Brace & World, 1964).

"Dating Play Premières"——Judith Milhous and Robert D. Hume, "Dating Play Premières from Publication Data, 1660-1700," *Harvard Library Bulletin*, 22 (1974), 374-405.

"Dr. Edward Browne's Playlists"——Robert D. Hume, "Dr. Edward Browne's Playlists of '1662': A Reconsideration," *Philological Quarterly*, 64 (1985), 69-81.

Dramatic Records of Sir Henry Herbert——*The Dramatic Records of Sir Henry Herbert*, ed. Joseph Quincy Adams (New Haven: Yale Univ. Press, 1917).

Fitzgerald——Percy Fitzgerald, *A New History of the English Stage*, 2 vols. (London: Tinsley, 1882).

Gildon——Charles Gildon, *The Life of Mr. Thomas Betterton* (London: Robert Gosling, 1710).

Hotson——Leslie Hotson, *The Commonwealth and Restoration Stage* (Cambridge: Harvard Univ. Press, 1928).

Knight——*Roscius Anglicanus*, reprinted in facsimile "With an Historical Preface" by Joseph Knight (London: J. W. Jarvis & Son, 1886).

Langbaine——Gerard Langbaine, *An Account of the English Dramatick Poets* (Oxford: L.L. for George West and Henry Clements, 1691).

The London Stage——*The London Stage, 1660-1800*, Part 1: 1660-1700, ed. William Van Lennep, Emmett L. Avery, and Arthur H. Scouten (Carbondale: Southern Illinois Univ. Press, 1965). Part 2: 1700-1729, ed. Emmett L. Avery, 2 vols. (1960).

LC (Lord Chamberlain)——Lord Chamberlain's records (at the Public Record Office unless otherwise specified).

"Lost English Plays"——Judith Milhous and Robert D. Hume, "Lost English Plays, 1660-1700," *Harvard Library Bulletin*, 25 (1977), 5-33.

Luttrell——Narcissus Luttrell, *A Brief Historical Relation of State Affairs*, 6 vols. (Oxford: University Press, 1857).

Milhous, *Thomas Betterton*——Judith Milhous, *Thomas Betterton and the Management of Lincoln's Inn Fields, 1695-1708* (Carbondale: Southern Illinois Univ. Press, 1979).

Nicoll——Allardyce Nicoll, *A History of English Drama, 1660-1900*, 6 vols., rev. ed. (Cambridge: Cambridge Univ. Press, 1952-1959).

Pepys——*The Diary of Samuel Pepys*, ed. Robert Latham and William Matthews, 11 vols. (London: Bell, 1970-1983).

P.R.O.——Public Record Office (London).

Summers——*Roscius Anglicanus*, ed. Montague Summers (London: Fortune Press, [1928]).

Vice Chamberlain Coke's Theatrical Papers——*Vice Chamberlain Coke's Theatrical Papers, 1706-1715*, ed. Judith Milhous and Robert D. Hume (Carbondale: Southern Illinois Univ. Press, 1982).

Waldron——*Roscius Anglicanus*, "With Additions, By the late Mr. Thomas Davies," ed. F. G. Waldron (London: Egerton, et al., 1789).

Wilson, *All the King's Ladies*——John Harold Wilson, *All the King's Ladies* (Chicago: Univ. of Chicago Press, 1958).

Roscius Anglicanus,

or an

HISTORICAL

Review of the

STAGE:

After it had been Suppres'd by means of the late Unhappy Civil War, begun in 1641, till the Time of King *Charles* the II^s. Restoration in *May* 1660. Giving an Account of its Rise again; of the Time and Places the Governours of both the Companies first Erected their Theatres.

The Names of the Principal Actors and Actresses, who Perform'd in the Chiefest Plays in each House. With the Names of the most taking Plays; and Modern Poets. For the space of 46 Years, and during the Reign of Three Kings, and part of our present Sovereign Lady Queen *ANNE*, from 1660, to 1706.

Non Audita narro, sed Comperta.[1]

London, Printed and sold by *H. Playford*, at his House in *Arundel-street*, near the Water-side, 1708.

---

[1] "I relate not hearsay, but experience."

[A2]

TO THE READER.

The Editor of the ensuing Relation, being long Conversant with the Plays and Actors of the Original Company, under the Patent of Sir *William Davenant*, at his Theatre in *Lincolns-Inn-Fields*, Open'd there *1662*.[2] And as Book-keeper[3] and Prompter, continu'd so, till *October 1706*.[4] He Writing out all the Parts in each Play; and Attending every Morning the Actors Rehearsals, and their Performances in Afternoons;[5] Emboldens him to affirm, he is not very Erronious in his Relation. But as to the Actors of *Drury-Lane* Company,

[A2v]

under Mr. *Thomas Killigrew*, he having the Account from Mr. *Charles Booth* sometimes Book-keeper there;[6] If he a little Deviates, as to the Successive Order, and exact time of their Plays Performances, He begs Pardon of the Reader, and Subscribes himself,

His very Humble Servant,

John Downes.

---

[2] *Recte* late June 1661 (Pepys).

[3] Librarian and keeper of promptbooks, not financial clerk (Summers, pp. 63-64).

[4] Downes was evidently forced into retirement at the time of the proto-union of September 1706. For details of that union, see Milhous, *Thomas Betterton*, pp. 207-215.

[5] In the 1660s performances began at 3:30; by the nineties the customary time had become 4:00. Around the turn of the century it became 5:00, 5:30, and even 6:00. See *The London Stage*, Part 1, pp. lxix-lxx. Rehearsals seem to have started at 10:00, and performances followed a break for a mid-afternoon dinner. See anon., *The Female Wits* (1696; pub. 1704), p. 1, and Buckingham, *The Rehearsal* (pub. 1672), p. 52 (i.e., p. 53).

[6] We know nothing of Charles Booth other than what Downes tells us in this passage. See *Biographical Dictionary*, II, 228.

[1]

Roscius Anglicanus,
or an
Historical Review
of the
STAGE.

In the Reign of King *Charles* the First, there were Six Play Houses allow'd in Town:[7] The *Black-Fryars* Company, His Majesty's Servants; The Bull[8] in St. *John's-street*; another in *Salisbury Court*;[9] another call'd the *Fortune*; another at the *Globe*; and the Sixth at the Cock-Pit in *Drury-Lane*;[10] all which continu'd Acting till the beginning of the said Civil Wars. The scattered Remnant of several of these Houses, upon King *Charles*'s Restoration, Fram'd a Company who Acted again at the Bull, and Built them a New

---

[7] For a general account of the Caroline theatres, see Bentley, Vol. VI.

[8] The Red Bull, used in the summer and early autumn of 1660 by the nucleus of the group that became the King's Company and occasionally by Jolly's troupe and unlicensed groups in the first years after the Restoration. See William Van Lennep, "The Death of the Red Bull," *Theatre Notebook*, 16 (1962), 126-134.

[9] Sir Henry Herbert issued (or at least drafted) a license to William Beeston for this theatre at an unknown date (traditionally said to be June 1660). The text is preserved in British Library Add. MS 19,256, fol. 100 (printed from an intermediary source in *The Dramatic Records of Sir Henry Herbert*, p. 81). Salisbury Court was definitely used by Davenant's Company in 1660-61 prior to the opening of Lincoln's Inn Fields.

[10] Occupied by Rhodes' Company in the spring and summer of 1660. Used by the King's Company prior to 8 November 1660 and probably by Jolly in the spring of 1661 (see "Dr. Edward Browne's Playlists"). Not to be confused with the Cockpit in Court.

House in *Gibbon's Tennis-Court* in *Clare-Market*;[11] in which Two
Places they continu'd Acting all 1660, 1661, 1662 and part of 1663.
In this time they Built them a New Theatre in *Drury Lane*:[12] Mr.
Thomas Killigrew gaining a Patent from the King in

[2]

order to Create them the King's Servants; and from that time, they
call'd themselves his Majesty's Company of Comedians[13] in *Drury-
Lane*.

Whose Names were, *viz.*[14]

Mr. *Theophilus Bird*.[15]	Mr. *Robert Shatterel*.
Mr. *Hart*.	Mr. *William Shatterel*.[16]

---

[11] The Vere Street theatre, opened 8 November 1660.

[12] The Bridges Street theatre, opened 7 May 1663—a changeable scenery theatre built by the King's Company to compete with Davenant's Lincoln's Inn Fields.

[13] Killigrew's patent passed the Great Seal 25 April 1662. The official roll-copy is P.R.O. C66/3013, no. 20. What appears to be Killigrew's exemplification is preserved in the Theatre Museum, Covent Garden (on loan from the Drury Lane theatre). The text is printed by Fitzgerald, I, 77-80.

[14] Twelve of these sixteen actors were sworn as Household servants to Charles II on 6 October 1660 (LC 3/25, p. 157): Burt, Hart, Mohun, Robert Shatterell, Lacy, Wintershall, Clun, Cartwright, Edward Shatterell, Kynaston, Baxter, and Marmaduke Watson. For the others, see notes on individuals.

[15] Bird was not sworn until 17 December 1661 (LC 3/26, p. 212—as a Queen's Comedian). We have no definite proof of his activity with the company until autumn 1661, but he could have joined any time after October 1660. He is often confused with Theophilus Bird, Jr., who performed with the King's Company from at least 1664-65 through 1673-74.

[16] Evidently an error for Edward Shatterell, whose name is frequently

Mr. *Mohun.*	Mr. *Duke.*[17]
Mr. *Lacy.*	Mr. *Hancock.*[18]
Mr. *Burt.*	Mr. *Kynaston.*
Mr. *Cartwright.*	Mr. *Wintersel.*
Mr. *Clun.*	Mr. *Bateman.*[19]

given in livery warrants and swearing-in rosters. Despite his well-documented presence in the company from 1660 to ca. 1667, his only known role is the King of Spain in Shirley's *The Court Secret*, revived ca. 1661-1664. See Judith Milhous and Robert D. Hume, "Manuscript Casts for Revivals of Three Plays by Shirley in the 1660s," *Theatre Notebook*, 39 (1985), 32-36. Our last record of him is his cancelled name in a livery warrant, P.R.O. LC 5/138, p. 271, dated 8 February 1667[/8?].

[17] I.e., Marmaduke Watson, who was sworn with the other original actors on 6 October 1660.

[18] Thomas Hancock was apparently not sworn until ca. 12 November 1664 (LC 3/25, p. 157), but his name appears in a livery warrant as early as 30 May 1662 (LC 5/138, p. 10), so he must have been active with the company by that spring (and perhaps earlier in female roles). See *Biographical Dictionary*, VII, 68.

[19] Thomas Bateman is entered in *The London Stage* and the *Biographical Dictionary* on the basis of a performance of *The Alchemist* in December 1660, but the cast is from Downes and the evidence for performance untrustworthy (see note 43 on *The Alchemist*, below). According to the manuscript cast for Shirley's *The Cardinal* in the Brotherton Collection (University of Leeds), a "Bateman" was active with the company before Clun's death in August 1664 and probably prior to that of Theophilus Bird, Senior (Bird broke a leg in September 1662 and died in March 1663). Whether there were one or two or three Batemans, and what his or their Christian names were, we cannot determine. For discussion of the "Bateman" problem, see Milhous and Hume, "Manuscript Casts" (note 16, above).

Mr. *Baxter*.   Mr. *Blagden*.[20]

Note, these following came not into the Company, till after they had begun in *Drury-Lane*.[21]

Mr. *Hains*.   These Four were Bred

Mr. *Griffin*.   up from Boys,[22] under the

Mr. *Goodman*.   Master Actors.

Mr. *Lyddoll*.[23]   Mr. *Bell*.

---

[20] Nicholas Blagden was not sworn until ca. 12 November 1664 (LC 3/25, p. 157), but he was active with the company by December 1661. According to Downes, p. 48 below, he worked briefly for the Duke's Company the previous summer.

[21] I.e., the Theatre-Royal, Bridges Street, opened 7 May 1663. Jo Haines moved from the Nursery to the King's Company during the season of 1667-68; Philip Griffin definitely joined by spring 1673 (and perhaps by ca. 1670-71), as did Cardell Goodman; Edward Lydall possibly ca. 1661-62 and definitely by 1666-67; Peter Carlton by summer 1673; George Shirley by 1668-69. On "Beeston," see note 25, below.

[22] This statement is plausible but not provable. Our first definite record of Richard Bell and Thomas Reeves is in 1668; of William Hughes and William Harris in 1667. A reference to a "Hews" in *The Royall King* (possibly ca. 1661-62) may be to William Hughes' appearance in a female role. By 1667-68 all four were apparently able to play adult roles.

[23] Edward Lydall is listed in *The London Stage* (p. 36) for 1661-62 on the basis of a problematical MS cast for Heywood's *The Royall King*. The first certain record of Lydall is his swearing-in on 10 May 1666 (LC 3/25, p. 157), but he was presumably active with the company prior to the closing of the theatres during the plague. His first definitely datable role was in *The Change of Crownes* in April 1667.

Mr. *Charleton.*	Mr. *Reeves.*[24]
Mr. *Sherly.*	Mr. *Hughs.*
Mr. *Beeston.*[25]	Mr. *Harris.*

Women.[26]

---

[24] Waldron (p. 11) suggests from Downes' errata list in the original edition of 1708 that "Reeves" should be emended to "Knight," but Joseph Knight observes that the error in the errata is probably in the page number rather than in the name and that the problem concerns page 3 rather than page "2," in which case on page 3 we should read "Mrs. Reeves" for "Mrs. Knight" (Knight, pp. xxvi-xxvii). Thus "Mr. Reeves" appears to be correct here: the reference is presumably to Thomas Reeves (husband or brother of Anne Reeves?), known to have been active with the King's Company in 1668-69.

[25] We cannot be certain whether Downes' source is referring to William Beeston (ca. 1606-1682) or to his son George (*fl.* 1660?-1675). William apparently joined the King's Company by the season of 1664-65; George had definitely joined by 1667. *The London Stage* unfortunately assigns all "Beeston" roles to a nonexistent William Beeston, Jr. The *Biographical Dictionary*, I, 413-419, proves that both father and son were active, even though there is often no way to be certain which of them played a particular role.

[26] Katherine Mitchell Corey was sworn as a member of the King's Company under her maiden name on 27 March 1661 (LC 3/25, p. 159). Anne Marshall was sworn the previous day; Mrs. Eastland was sworn 27 March 1661 (though no definite roles are known for her until 1669); Elizabeth Farley Weaver joined under her maiden name in 1661; Mrs. Uphill is not recorded until 1669; Mrs. Knepp joined in autumn 1664 (unless she was the Mary Man sworn 27 March 1661); Margaret Hughes had joined by spring 1668; Rebecca Marshall was sworn on 27 March 1661, as was Margaret Rutter.

Mrs. *Corey*.	*Note*, these following
Mrs. *Ann Marshall*.	came into the Company
Mrs. *Eastland*.	some few Years after.[27]
Mrs. *Weaver*.	
Mrs. *Uphill*.	Mrs. *Boutel*.[28]
Mrs. *Knep*.	Mrs. *Ellin Gwin*.[29]

---

[27] Some few years after what is not clear—presumably the foundation of the company, not the opening of the Bridges Street theatre. The two columns are not clearly distinguished. Elizabeth Davenport (later Bowtell) probably joined ca. 1663-64 (see note 28, below); Gwyn was active by 1664 (see note 29); Elizabeth James was definitely performing by the winter of 1670; Verjuice and Reeves present special problems (see below).

[28] I.e., Elizabeth Davenport, who married Barnaby Bowtell during the season of 1669-70. See Judith Milhous, "Elizabeth Bowtell and Elizabeth Davenport: Some Puzzles Solved," *Theatre Notebook*, 39 (1985), 124-134. Davenport had definitely joined the company by March 1667, when she performed in Dryden's *Secret-Love*. If Downes' cast for *Rule a Wife* is accurate, then she had joined by 1663-64. See note 37, below.

[29] Though both John Harold Wilson and the editors of *The London Stage* assumed that Nell Gwyn took no lead roles until 1666-67, evidence that she did so prior to Clun's death in August 1664 has come to light. See K. Robinson, "Two Cast Lists for Buckingham's 'The Chances,'" *Notes and Queries*, 224 (1979), 436-437, and Douglas R. Butler, "The Date of Buckingham's Revision of *The Chances* and Nell Gwynn's First Season on the London Stage," *Notes and Queries*, 227 (1982), 515-516. Gwyn had evidently joined the King's Company by 1663-64. For a plausible argument that she was born in 1650 (rather than 1642), see David Bond, "Nell Gwyn's Birthdate," *Theatre Notebook*, 40 (1986), 3-9.

Mrs. *Hughs*. | Mrs. *James*.

[3]

Mrs. *Rebecca Marshall*. | Mrs. *Verjuice*.[30]

Mrs. *Rutter*. | Mrs. *Reeves*.[31]

The Company being thus Compleat,[32] they open'd the New Theatre in *Drury-Lane*, on *Thursday* in *Easter* Week, being the *8th*, Day of *April* 1663,[33] With the *Humorous Lieutenant*.
Note, this Comedy was Acted Twelve Days Successively.

I.[34]

---

[30] Unknown in any other source, and hence undatable.

[31] Downes' text says "Mrs. *Knight*." An Ursula Knight performed briefly with the company in 1676 and 1677; no definite record of Frances Maria Knight exists prior to 1684. Therefore we have accepted Joseph Knight's emendation of Downes' errata (see note 24, above) and have corrected "Knight" to "Reeves." Anne Reeves does not appear in the records until December 1670, but on chronological grounds she seems the most probable candidate. For discussion of the problems with Reeves' biography, see James A. Winn, "Dryden and Anne Reeves: Some Facts and Questions," *Restoration*, 10 (1986), 1-13.

[32] Downes' implication that the company he has just named was assembled for the opening of Bridges Street and immediately thereafter is rather misleading. Broadly speaking, however, it represents the King's Company's personnel of the 1660s.

[33] *Recte* 7 May 1663 (Pepys).

[34] On page 24 Downes terms the following group of fifteen plays "their Principal Old Stock Plays" (as opposed to those "Writ by the then *Modern Poets*"). This is not quite accurate, since he includes Dryden's *Secret-Love* (1667) and *An Evening's Love* (1668). Authorities have differed on the reli-

The Humorous Lieutenant.[35]

King,	Mr. *Wintersel.*
Demetrius,	Mr. *Hart.*
Seleucus,	Mr. *Burt.*
Leontius,	Major *Mohun.*
Lieutenant,	Mr. *Clun.*

---

ability of these casts, skeptics being particularly concerned about the presence of "Mrs. Boutel" in three of them. With the Bowtell problem solved, however, all the casts appear feasible, with the possible exception of *Julius Caesar*, where we have no other record of Mrs. Corbet as early as would be required for her to perform with Richard Bell. Plainly these casts are not always for the earliest performance after the Restoration, but they do appear plausible as reported. There is no longer any good reason to suppose that they are composites, even though in some cases (e.g., *The Elder Brother*) performance cannot be documented within the time span implied by Downes' cast. In each case we have tried to indicate the range of months or years over which Downes' cast would have been available.

[35] According to Downes, Fletcher's comedy (1619?) was played at the Red Bull in the summer and early autumn of 1660; by the King's Company at Vere Street on 29 November 1660. This cast could have been assembled at any time after "Mrs. Marshall" joined the company, an event that occurred between December 1660 (when the first actress appeared) and late March 1661 (when both of the Marshalls were sworn). With scenery, the play was used to open the Bridges Street theatre in May 1663. According to Pepys (8 May), Lacy replaced Clun as the Lieutenant in this production "by the King's command." The cast as given above therefore pertains to the period spring 1661 to spring 1663. Performances are known on 20 April 1661 and 1 March 1662.

Celia,	Mrs. *Marshal*.[36]

II.

Rule a Wife, and have a Wife.[37]

Don Leon,	Major *Mohun*.
Don John Decastrio,	Mr. *Burt*.
Michael Perez,	Mr. *Hart*.
Cacafago,	Mr. *Clun*.

---

[36] Probably Anne Marshall, rather than her sister Rebecca, though their roles cannot be distinguished with confidence. Downes (or his source) specifies "Mrs. Ann Marshall" only in the *Rule a Wife* cast. Hence some uncertainty must attach to all other "Marshall" roles through 1665, when Anne became Mrs. Quin. See Wilson, *All the King's Ladies*, pp. 168-172. Wilson believes that Rebecca took no major roles until 1666-67, when Pepys saw her, probably as Evadne, in *The Maid's Tragedy* on 7 December. Whether she took the role earlier or replaced her sister we do not know. But Rebecca had performed the role of Maria in Shirley's *The Court Secret* prior to August 1664 (see "Manuscript Casts," note 16, above).

[37] Fletcher's comedy (1624) was performed by Rhodes' Company at the Cockpit in 1660. It was temporarily allowed to the Duke's Company on 12 December 1660 (LC 5/137, pp. 343-344) and performed at Salisbury Court on 1 April 1661, but it was reclaimed by the King's Company and was in their repertory by 28 January 1662. The cast as given probably pertains to the season of 1663-64. Mrs. Bowtell (as Elizabeth Davenport) probably did not join the company much before this season, and Clun died in August 1664.

Margareta,	Mrs. *Ann Marshal.*
Estifania,	Mrs. *Boutell.*[38]

III.

The Fox.[39]

[4]

Volpone,	Major *Mohun.*
Mosca,	Mr. *Hart.*
Corbachio,	Mr. *Cartwright.*
Voltore,	Mr. *Shatterel.*
Corvino,	Mr. *Burt.*
Sir Politique Woud-be,	Mr. *Lacy.*

---

[38] I.e., Elizabeth Davenport. See note 28, above.

[39] Jonson's *Volpone* (1605-1606) was in the King's Company's repertory by October 1662. *The London Stage*, Part 1, p. 86, arbitrarily assigns Downes' cast to a performance in January 1665, but all the performers named would have been available by the spring of 1661, when Katherine Mitchell (later Corey) joined the company. If this Mrs. Marshall was Anne (as Wilson believes), then the cast as given probably pertains to the period before the closing of the theatres in June 1665, though Anne Marshall Quin performed with the King's Company in 1667 and 1668.

Peregrine,	Mr. *Kynaston*.
Lady Woud-be,	Mrs. *Corey*.
Celia,	Mrs. *Marshal*.[40]

IV.

The Silent Woman.[41]

Morose,	Mr. *Cartwright*.
True-Wit,	Major *Mohun*.
Cleremont,	Mr. *Burt*.
Dauphin,	Mr. *Kynaston*.
Sir Amorous,	Mr. *Wintersel*.
Sir John Daw,	Mr. *Shatterel*.
Captain Otter,	Mr. *Lacy*.
Epicene,	Mrs. *Knep*.[42]

---

[40] Probably Anne Marshall (later Quin), rather than her sister Rebecca, but see note 36, above.

[41] Jonson's play (1609) was performed (at the Red Bull?) as early as June 1660 and was in the King's Company's repertory by 10 November 1660. It seems to have been a stock play throughout the 1660s. This cast could have been assembled any time between autumn 1664 and 1677. Knepp apparently joined the company in 1664 and Rutter left in 1677.

[42] Summers comments at length on the peculiar tradition of a woman

| Lady Haughty, | Mrs. *Rutter*. |
| Mrs. Otter, | Mrs. *Corey*. |

V.

The Alchemist.[43]

Subtil,	Mr. *Wintersel*.
Face,	Major *Mohun*.
Sir Epicure Mammon,	Mr. *Cartwright*.
Surly,	Mr. *Burt*.
Ananias,	Mr. *Lacy*.

[5]

---

taking this role (pp. 104-105). When Pepys saw the play on 7 January 1661, Kynaston played Epicene.

[43] Jonson's comedy (1610) was definitely in the King's Company's repertory by June 1661 and was regularly performed thereafter. (The performance listed for December 1660 in *The London Stage* is based on arbitrary assignment of a broadside prologue that may date from the interregnum.) This cast probably pertains to the period autumn 1664 to 1669. All members might have been available as early as the spring of 1661. We do not know when Bateman joined; see note 19, above. On 17 April 1669 Pepys lamented the loss of Clun as Subtle. Wintershall evidently took over the role after his colleague's death in August 1664, so we are inclined to place this cast between that time and Bateman's disappearance from the records ca. 1669.

Wholesome,[44]	Mr. *Bateman.*
Dol. Common,	Mrs. *Corey.*
Dame Plyant,	Mrs. *Rutter.*

VI.

The Maids Tragedy.[45]

King,	Mr. *Wintersel.*
Melantius,	Major *Mohun.*
Amintor,	Mr. *Hart.*
Calianax,	Mr. *Shatterel.*
Evadne,	Mrs. *Marshal.*[46]

---

[44] I.e., Tribulation Wholesome (Waldron, pp. 13, 17).

[45] Beaumont and Fletcher's play (ca. 1608-1611) was performed at the Red Bull in the summer and early autumn of 1660 and was in the King's Company's repertory by 17 November. This cast evidently pertains to the period from 1663-64 (by which time Elizabeth Davenport, later Bowtell, was probably active) through spring 1677 (when Rebecca Marshall left the company). A manuscript cast in Folger Art Folio 271 that pre-dates actresses lists Wintershall as Evadne, Hart as Amintor, and Cartwright as Calianax. See David George, "Early Cast Lists for Two Beaumont and Fletcher Plays," *Theatre Notebook*, 28 (1974), 9-11.

[46] Rebecca Marshall (Pepys, 7 December 1666). But see note 36, above.

| Aspatia, | Mrs. *Boutel.*[47] |

VII.

King and no King.[48]

Arbaces,	Mr. *Hart.*
Tygranes,	Mr. *Burt.*
Mardonius,	Major *Mohun.*
Gobrias,	Mr. *Wintersel.*
Lygones,	Mr. *Cartwright.*
Bessus,	Mr. *Shotterel.*
Arane,	Mrs. *Corey.*
Panthea,	Madam *Gwin.*

---

[47] Elizabeth Davenport (see note 28, above).

[48] Beaumont and Fletcher's play (1611) was performed at the Red Bull in the summer and early autumn of 1660 and was in the King's Company's repertory by 3 December 1660. This cast would have been available between the season of 1663-64 (when Nell Gwyn began to take significant roles) and spring 1671 (when she left the stage). A cast available during the early to mid-seventies is printed in Q1676: Arbaces—Hart; Tygranes—Kynaston; Gobrias—Wintershall; Bacurius—Lydal; Mardonius—Mohun; Bessus—Lacy or Shottrell; Lygones—Cartwright; Two Swordsmen—Watson, Haynes; Arane—Mrs. Corey; Panthea—Mrs. Cox; Spaconia—Mrs. Marshall.

VIII.

Rollo, Duke of Normandy.[49]

Rollo,	Mr. *Hart.*
Otto,	Mr. *Kynaston.*
Aubrey,	Major *Mohun.*

[6]

La Torch,	Mr. *Burt.*
Dutchess,	Mrs. *Corey.*
Edith,	Mrs. *Marshal.*

IX.

---

[49] Fletcher, Massinger, and Jonson's (?) *Rollo, Duke of Normandy, or The Bloody Brother* (ca. 1616-1624) was performed at the Red Bull in the summer and early autumn of 1660 and was in the King's Company's repertory by 6 December. All of the performers named by Downes would have been available by late in the season of 1660-61, perhaps as early as mid-December. This cast was probably responsible for the performance at Bridges Street ca. October 1663 attended by Edward Browne (not in *The London Stage* under date); see "Dr. Edward Browne's Playlists." The *terminus ad quem* for this cast is uncertain. Anne Marshall ceased to perform under that name after June 1665 but remained with the company under her married name, Quin, until summer 1668. Rebecca Marshall left the company in the spring of 1677.

The Scornful Lady.[50]

Elder Loveless,	Mr. *Burt.*
Younger Loveless,	Mr. *Kynaston.*
Welford,	Mr. *Hart.*
Sir Roger,	Mr. *Lacy.*
The Lady,	Mrs. *Marshal.*
Martha,	Mrs. *Rutter.*
Abigail,	Mrs. *Corey.*

X.

The Elder Brother.[51]

---

[50] Fletcher's play (ca. 1613-1616) was in the King's Company's repertory by 21 November 1660. The cast as given would have been available by the spring of 1661 and would have remained so until the retirement of whichever Marshall performed the Lady—i.e., 1668 or 1677. We should note, however, that Pepys reports Mrs. Knepp as the Lady on 27 December 1666 and implies that she took the part again on 3 June 1668. This may mean that the role belonged to Anne Marshall and that the cast is for performances prior to the closing of the theatres in June 1665.

[51] Fletcher and Massinger's play (1625?) was performed at the Red Bull in the summer and early autumn of 1660 and was in the King's Company's repertory by 23 November 1660. The cast as given probably pertains to the period ca. 1663-64 to 1669. The limiting factors are the unknown date at which Elizabeth Davenport Bowtell joined the company

Charles,	Mr. *Burt.*
Eustace,	Mr. *Kynaston.*
Their Father,[52]	Mr. *Loveday.*
The Uncle,	Mr. *Gradwel.*
Charles's Man,	Mr. *Shotterel.*
Lady,	Mrs. *Rutter.*
Lilia Bianca,[53]	Mrs. *Boutel.*[54]

XI.

The Moor of Venice.[55]

and the disappearance of Gradwell and Loveday from the records by the autumn of 1669. (They do not appear in a livery warrant of 2 October.) No definite performance dates for the play are known in this span.

[52] Summers (p. 109) fills in the character names: the father is Brisac; the uncle is Miramont; Charles's Man is Andrew; the Lady is Angellina.

[53] As Summers observes, Lilia Bianca is a character in *The Wild Goose Chase*, a role Bowtell may also have played. Her part in *The Elder Brother* was evidently Lilly, Andrew's wife.

[54] Elizabeth Davenport Bowtell (see note 28, above).

[55] *Othello* (ca. 1603-1604) was performed at the Red Bull in the summer and early autumn of 1660 and at the Cockpit in Drury Lane in October. It was performed by the King's Company at Vere Street on 8 December 1660, with "A Prologue to introduce the first Woman that came to Act on the Stage in the Tragedy, call'd *The Moor of Venice.*" See Thomas Jordan, *A Royal Arbor of Loyal Poesie* (London: R. Wood for Eliz. Andrews, 1664), pp. 21-22. Who performed Desdemona in 1660 has been hotly

Brabantio,	Mr. *Cartwright.*
Moor,	Mr. *Burt.*
Cassio,	Mr. *Hart.*[56]

[7]

Jago,	Major *Mohun.*[57]
Roderigo,	Mr. *Beeston.*[58]

---

debated, but unfortunately there is no substantial evidence. See Wilson, *All the King's Ladies,* pp. 5-8. Since Margaret Hughes seems to have joined the King's Company in spring 1668 and left in 1670, the cast as given evidently belongs to the brief intervening period. A performance is recorded at Bridges Street on 6 February 1669.

[56] Pepys confirms that Cassio was Hart's role (6 February 1669, when "another" played it). Eighteenth-century tradition seems to have held that "*Mr. Hart* became soon so superior to *Burt,* that he took the lead of him in almost all the Plays acted at Drury-Lane; *Othello* was one of his master-parts" (Davies, in the Waldron edition, p. 15). The edition of 1681 lists Hart as Othello; Burt remained active with the company until about 1678. All of the performers recorded in the edition of 1681 would have been available for the known performance on 25 January 1675. Thus the evidence makes Davies' assertion plausible, though it does not actually prove that Hart displaced Burt while the latter was still active.

[57] Michael Mohun evidently replaced Clun as Iago after Clun's death in August 1664. *An Elegy Upon the Most Execrable Murther of Mr. Clun* (1664) implies that Iago had been one of his most effective roles. See G. Thorn-Drury, *A Little Ark* (London: Dobell, 1921), pp. 30-32. Pepys found Mohun much inferior in the part on 6 February 1669.

[58] Whether this is William Beeston or his son George we cannot be certain. See note 25, above.

| Desdemona, | Mrs. *Hughs.* |
| Emilia, | Mrs. *Rutter.* |

XII.

King Henry the Fourth.[59]

King,	Mr. *Wintersel.*
Prince,	Mr. *Burt.*
Hotspur,	Mr. *Hart.*
Falstaff,	Mr. *Cartwright.*[60]
Poyns,	Mr. *Shotterel.*

XIII.

---

[59] Shakespeare's play (ca. 1596-1598) was the work with which the King's Company opened at Vere Street on 8 November 1660, and it seems to have been played often ever after. The cast as named would have been available from October 1660 to about 1678, when Burt ceased to perform—but see the next note.

[60] *An Elegy Upon the Most Execrable Murther of Mr. Clun* identifies Falstaff as one of his principal parts. Cartwright had taken over the role by 2 November 1667 (Pepys). He was evidently succeeded in the part by John Lacy (*d.* September 1681) at an unknown date. Langbaine reports that Falstaff "used to be play'd by Mr. *Lacy,* and never fail'd of universal applause" (p. 456).

The Maiden Queen.[61]

Lysimantes,	Mr. *Burt.*
Philocles,	Major *Mohun.*
Celadon,	Mr. *Hart.*
Queen,	Mrs. *Marshal.*
Asteria,	Mrs. *Knep.*
Florimel,	Mrs. *Elen. Gwin.*
Melissa,	Mrs. *Corey.*

XIV.

Mock Astrologer.[62]

---

[61] Dryden's *Secret-Love, or The Maiden Queen*, premièred ca. late February 1667. This cast, evidently that of the first production, is confirmed by Q1668, which adds: Candiope—Mrs. Quin; Flavia—Frances Davenport; Olinda—Mrs. Rutter; Sabina—Elizabeth Davenport. The part of this cast reported by Downes would have been available until Nell Gwyn left the stage in 1671.

[62] Dryden's *An Evening's Love, or the Mock-Astrologer*, premièred in June 1668. The cast reported by Downes would have been available at that time and remained so until Margaret Hughes left the stage in 1670. When the play was published in 1671, Mrs. Bowtell was listed as Theodosia in place of Mrs. Hughes. For Aurelia the quarto gives "Mrs. *Marshall*; and formerly by Mrs. *Quin*"—i.e., Rebecca Marshall had replaced her sister by 1671. Q1671 also adds: Don Melchor—Lydall; Beatrix—Knepp;

Don Alonzo,	Mr. *Wintersel.*
Don Lopez,	Mr. *Burt.*
Belamy,	Major *Mohun.*
Wildblood,	Mr. *Hart.*

[8]

Maskal,	Mr. *Shatterel.*
Theodosia,	Mrs. *Hughs.*
Jacyntha,	Mrs. *Elen. Gwin.*
Aurelia,	Mrs. *Quyn.*

XV.

Julius Cæsar.[63]

Camilla—Betty Slate (i.e., Slade). All of them would probably have been available for the première.

[63] The first definite performance date for Shakespeare's tragedy (ca. 1598-1600) in this period is 4 December 1676. However, the *Covent Garden Drollery* of 1672 includes a prologue for it, and Downes' cast can be no later than 25 January 1671/2, when Richard Bell lost his life in the fire that destroyed the Bridges Street theatre. (Cardell Goodman took the role of Caesar at an unknown later date.) Mrs. Corbett has no proven roles until January 1675, but Portia speaks in only one scene, so the actress would not have needed much experience. By this time "Mrs. Marshall" is

Julius Cæsar,	Mr. *Bell*.
Cassius,	Major *Mohun*.
Brutus,	Mr. *Hart*.
Anthony,	Mr. *Kynaston*.
Calphurnia,	Mrs. *Marshal*.
Portia,	Mrs. *Corbet*.

Note, That these being their Principal Old Stock Plays;[64] yet in this Interval from the Day they begun, there were divers others Acted,[65] As

---

presumably Rebecca. For discussion of the highly problematical MS cast written in British Library C.131.c.14 (Q1691), see Edward A. Langhans, "New Restoration Manuscript Casts," *Theatre Notebook*, 27 (1973), 149-157, esp. 151-152. In *"Julius Caesar* and Restoration Shakespeare," *Shakespeare Quarterly*, 29 (1978), 423-427, Arthur H. Scouten offers the plausible hypothesis that this cast is a composite reflecting three distinct productions, ca. 1663-64, ca. 1668-1672, and ca. 1674-1677. Downes' cast is clearly for the second of these.

[64] For the best discussion of pre-1642 drama in the repertories of the King's and Duke's companies, see Gunnar Sorelius, *'The Giant Race Before the Flood': Pre-Restoration Drama on the Stage and in the Criticism of the Restoration*, Studia Anglistica Upsaliensia, 4 (Uppsala: Almqvist & Wiksells, 1966). On the vexed question of the rights of the two companies to old plays, see Gunnar Sorelius, "The Rights of the Restoration Theatrical Companies in the Older Drama," *Studia Neophilologica*, 37 (1965), 174-189, and Robert D. Hume, "Securing a Repertory: Plays on the London Stage 1660-5," *Poetry and Drama 1570-1700: Essays in Honour of Harold F. Brooks*, ed. Antony Coleman and Antony Hammond (London: Methuen, 1981), pp. 156-172.

[65] Of the twenty-one plays in the following list, all but *The Carnival* date from before the closing of the theatres in 1642. Downes is our only

Cataline's Conspiracy.
The Merry Wives of Windsor.
The Opportunity.
The Example.
The Jovial Crew.
Philaster.
The Cardinal.
Bartholomew-Fair.
The Chances.
The Widow.
The Devil's an Ass.
Argulus and Parthenia.
Every Man in his Humour.
Every Man out of Humour.
The Carnival.
Sejanus.

[9]

The Merry Devil of Edmunton.
Vittoria Corumbona.
The Beggars Bush.
The Traytor.
Titus Andronicus.

These being Old Plays, were Acted but now and then; yet being well Perform'd, were very Satisfactory to the Town.

Next follow the Plays, Writ by the then *Modern Poets*, As,

---

evidence of revival for *The Example, Sejanus,* and *Titus Andronicus.* In all but three of the rest of the cases, we have evidence of revival between 1660 and 1665: *Catiline* was apparently not revived until 1667; *Every Man in His Humour* and *Every Man out of His Humour* are not recorded until 1670 and 1675 respectively. For details, see Endnote 1.

The Indian Emperour.[66]

Emperour,	Major *Mohun.*
Odmar,	Mr. *Wintersel.*
Guymor,	Mr. *Kynaston.*
Priest,	Mr. *Cartwright.*
Cortez,	Mr. *Hart.*
Vasquez,	Mr. *Burt.*
Cidaria,	Mrs. *Ellen Gwin.*[67]
Almeria,	Mrs. *Marshall.*

Plain Dealer.[68]

---

[66] Dryden's play was premièred ca. February-March 1665 (estimated from publication). Downes' cast would have been available at that time. Q1667 contains no actors' names. If Almeria was played by Anne Marshall (later Quin), then this cast would not have been available after summer 1668; if Rebecca Marshall took the part, then the *terminus ad quem* is supplied by Nell Gwyn's final departure from the stage in 1671.

[67] *The London Stage* says that Gwyn "probably was not in the original cast" (p. 87), but the hypothesis on which this assertion rests has since been disproved. See note 29, above.

[68] Wycherley's play received its première in December 1676. Q1677 confirms this cast, which would have been available only until Rebecca Marshall's departure from the King's Company ca. April 1677. Q1677 adds: Letice—Mrs. [Ursula?] Knight.

Manly,	Mr. *Hart.*
Freeman,	Mr. *Kynaston.*
Vernish,	Mr. *Griffin.*[69]
Novel,	Mr. *Clark.*
Major Oldfox,	Mr. *Cartwright.*
Lord Plausible,	Mr. *Haines.*

[10]

Jerry Blackacre,	Mr. *Charleton.*

Women:

Olivia,	Mrs. *Marshall.*
Fidelia,	Mrs. *Boutel.*
Eliza,	Mrs. *Knep.*
Widow Blackacre,	Mrs. *Corey.*

---

[69] At an unknown date Philip Griffin replaced Hart as Manly (see below, p. 85).

Tyrannick Love.[70]

Maximin,	Major *Mohun.*
Porphyrius,	Mr. *Hart.*
Placidius,	Mr. *Kynaston.*
Nigrinus,	Mr. *Beeston.*
Amariel,	Mr. *Bell.*
Charinus,	Mr. *Harris.*
Valerius,	Mr. *Lydal.*
Albinus,	Mr. *Littlewood.*
Apollonius,	Mr. *Cartwright.*

Women.

[70] Dryden's tragedy received its première in June 1669. Downes' cast evidently reflects performances in the season of 1670-71. According to the first quarto (1670), the part of St. Catharine was created by Margaret Hughes, who left the stage in 1670 and was replaced by Bowtell. A terminal date is supplied by Nell Gwyn's departure in 1671. Q1670 adds: Felicia—Mrs. Knep; Erotion—Mrs. Uphill; Cydnon—Mrs. Eastland. On the evidence of the *Roscius Anglicanus* cast, Mrs. Knepp doubled Felicia (Saint Catharine's mother) and Nakar (an aerial spirit who takes part in the vision scene in Act IV). Nakar and Damilcar are omitted from the cast list in Q1670.

Empress,	Mrs. *Marshall.*
Valeria,	Mrs. *Ellin Gwin.*
St. Catherine,	Mrs. *Boutel.*
Nacur,	Mrs. *Knep.*
Damilcar,	Mrs. *James.*

Aureng Zeb.[71]

Old Emperour,	Major *Mohun.*
Aureng Zeb *his Son,*	Mr. *Hart.*
Morat *the Younger Son,*	Mr. *Kynaston.*
Arimant,	Mr. *Wintersel.*

[11]

Women.

---

[71] Dryden's *Aureng-Zebe* was first performed in November 1675. Q1676 confirms Downes' cast as that of the original production. It probably remained available until Rebecca Marshall's departure from the company ca. April 1677, though Mrs. Cox may have left the company for several years as early as the autumn of 1676. Q1676 adds: Zayda—Mrs. Uphil.

Nourmahal *the Empress*,	Mrs. *Marshal*.
Indamora,	Mrs. *Cox*.
Melesinda,	Mrs. *Corbet*.

Alexander the Great.[72]

Alexander,	Mr. *Hart*.
Clytus,	Major *Mohun*.
Lysimachus,	Mr. *Griffin*.
Hephestion,	Mr. *Clark*.
Cassander,	Mr. *Kynaston*.
Polyperchon,	Mr. *Goodman*.

Women.

| Sysigambis, | Mrs. *Corey*. |
| Statyra, | Mrs. *Boutell*. |

---

[72] Nathaniel Lee's *The Rival Queens*, premièred 17 March 1677. This cast (confirmed by Q1677) pertains only to the original production, since Rebecca Marshall left the company the next month. The quarto adds: Philip—Powell; Thessalus—Wiltshire; Perdiccas—Lydall; Eumenes—Watson; Meleager—Perin; Aristander—Coysh; Parisatis—Mrs. Baker.

Roxana,	Mrs. *Marshall.*

All for Love, or the World well Lost.[73]

Marc Anthony,	Mr. *Hart.*
Ventidius *his General,*	Major *Mohun.*
Dolabella *his Friend,*	Mr. *Clark.*
Alexas *the Queens Eunuch,*	Mr. *Goodman.*
Seraphion,	Mr. *Griffin.*

Women.

Cleopatra,	Mrs. *Boutell.*
Octavia,	Mrs. *Corey.*

[12]

---

[73] Dryden's tragedy received its première by December 1677. This cast was available at that time. It is confirmed by Q1678, which adds: Another Priest—Coysh. How long these performers were available is uncertain. Bowtell left the stage sometime after February 1678; Clark and Goodman went to Edinburgh late in 1678 or early in 1679 (see Hotson, p. 262).

The Assignation, or Love in a Nunnery.[74]

Duke of Mantua,	Major *Mohun.*
Prince Frederick,	Mr. *Kynaston.*
Aurelian,	Mr. *Hart.*
Camillo *his Friend,*	Mr. *Burt.*
Mario,	Mr. *Cartwright.*
Ascanio *Page,*	Mrs. *Reeves.*[75]
Benito,	Mr. *Haines.*

Women.

Sophronia,	Mrs. *James.*
Lucretia,	Mrs. *Marshall.*
Hyppolita *a Nun,*	Mrs. *Knep.*

---

[74] Dryden's comedy apparently received its première between late spring and ca. November 1672. Q1673 confirms this as the cast of the original production. With some gaps caused by Haines' wanderings, it would have been available until Anne Reeves left the stage in 1675, assuming that she took Ascanio (see note below). On the issue of whether this was a "taking" play, see *The Works of John Dryden,* vol. XI, ed. John Loftis, et al. (Berkeley: Univ. of California Press, 1978), p. 507.

[75] The 1708 edition of *Roscius Anglicanus* reads "Mr. Reeves," but Q1673 says "Mrs. Reeve"—i.e., Anne Reeves.

| Laura, | Mrs. *Boutel.* |
| Violetta, | Mrs. *Cox.* |

Mythridates King of Pontus.[76]

Mythridates,	Major *Mohun.*
Ziphares,	Mr. *Hart.*
Pharnaces,	Mr. *Goodman.*
Archelaus,	Mr. *Griffin.*
Pelopidus,	Mr. *Wintersel.*
Aquilius,	Mr. *Clark.*

Women.

| Monima, | Mrs. *Corbet.* |
| Semandra, | Mrs. *Boutel.* |

[13]

---

[76] Lee's tragedy received its première ca. February 1678. Q1678 confirms this cast and adds: Andravar—Powell; Roman Officer—Wiltshire. We cannot be certain how long this cast was available. The *Mithridates* quarto is the last record of Bowtell's acting until 1688; Clark and Goodman went to Edinburgh in 1678-79; and we have no record of Mrs. Corbett between March 1678 and May 1681.

The Destruction of Jerusalem.[77]

Titus Vespasian,	Mr. *Kynaston.*
Phraartes,	Mr. *Hart.*
Matthias *high Priest*,	Major *Mohun.*
John,	Mr. *Cartwright.*

Women.

Clarona *Daughter to* Matthias,	Mrs. *Boutell.*
Queen Berenice,	Mrs. *Marshall.*

---

[77] Crowne's play, in two parts, received its première in January 1677. This cast would have been available for the first production but not after ca. April, when Rebecca Marshall left the company. Q1677 does not identify actors in the Dramatis Personae list but names Marshall in the headnote to the epilogue for Part II. Crowne had been under contract to the Duke's Company, and (according to a King's Company petition the next year protesting the desertion of Dryden and Lee) the King's Company was heavily penalized for producing this play. See James M. Osborn, *John Dryden: Some Biographical Facts and Problems*, 2nd ed. (Gainesville: Univ. of Florida Press, 1965), pp. 200-207.

Marriage Alamode.[78]

Polydamus,	Mr. *Wintersel.*
Leonidas,	Mr. *Kynaston.*
Harmogenes,	Mr. *Cartwright.*
Rhodophil,	Major *Mohun.*
Palamede,	Mr. *Burt.*

Women.

Palmira,	Mrs. *Cox.*
Amathea,	Mrs. *James.*
Doralice,	Mrs. *Marshall.*
Melantha,	Mrs. *Boutell.*

---

[78] Dryden's play was first produced ca. December 1671. See Robert D. Hume, "The Date of Dryden's *Marriage A-la-Mode*," *Harvard Library Bulletin*, 21 (1973), 161-166. Downes' cast would have been available from the première to the spring of 1677, when Rebecca Marshall left the company. Q1673 confirms most of this cast and adds: Argaleon—Lydall; Eubulus—Watson; Philotis—Mrs. Reeve; Belisa—Mrs. Slade; Artemis—Mrs. Uphill. Q1673 also gives: Palamede—Hart. The role seems more in keeping with Hart's line than with Burt's, and according to the *Covent Garden Drollery* (1672) Hart spoke the prologue. Whether "Burt" is an error or whether he took the role sometime between 1672 and 1678 (when he evidently retired), we have no way to determine.

The Unhappy Favourite, or the Earl of Essex.[79]

The Earl of Essex,	Mr. *Clark.*
The Earl of Southampton,	Mr. *Griffin.*
Lord Burleigh,	Major *Mohun.*

[14]

Women.

Queen Elizabeth,	Mrs. *Gwin.*[80]
Countess of Rutland,	Mrs. *Cook.*
Countess of Nottingham,	Mrs. *Corbet.*

The Black Prince.[81]

---

[79] Banks' tragedy was first performed ca. early April 1681. This cast was available from the première to the spring of 1682, when the company collapsed. Q1682 adds: Sir Walter Rawleigh—Disney.

[80] For Queen Elizabeth Q1682 gives: Mrs. Quyn. This implies that Anne Marshall Quin returned to the King's Company about this time.

[81] Orrery's play received its première 19 October 1667. The first edition (1672) confirms Downes' cast as that of the first production and adds: Page—[George?] Beeston; Sevina—Mrs. Nepp. This cast would have been available only until Frances Davenport's departure from the stage in April 1668.

King Edward the 3*d*,	Major *Mohun*.
King John *of* France,	Mr. *Wintersel*.
The Black Prince,	Mr. *Kynaston*.
Lord Delaware,	Mr. *Hart*.
Count Gueselin,	Mr. *Burt*.
Lord Latimer,	Mr. *Cartwright*.

Women.

Alizia,	Mrs. *Gwin*.[82]
Plantagenet,	Mrs. *Marshall*.
Cleorin,	Mrs. *Corey*.
Valeria *Disguis'd*,	F. *Damport*.[83]
A Lady,	Betty *Damport*.[84]

---

[82] The edition of 1672 gives "Mrs. Guinn." The editors of *The London Stage* assume that Nell Gwyn took the part, and they index it that way. John Harold Wilson says flatly that Anne Marshall Quin played the role (*All the King's Ladies*, p. 169). Alizia is more in Quin's line than Gwyn's, and the authors of the *Biographical Dictionary* feel that lack of comment from Pepys (with whom Nell was a favourite) tips the probability toward Mrs. Quin. No definite conclusion is possible.

[83] I.e., Frances Davenport.

[84] I.e., Elizabeth Davenport, later Bowtell.

The Conquest of Granada, 2 Parts.[85]

Mahomet Boabdelin	Mr. *Kynaston.*
last King of Granada,	
Prince Abdalla,	Mr. *Lydal.*
Abdemelech,	Major *Mohun.*
Abenamar,	Mr. *Cartwright.*
Almanzer,	Mr. *Hart.*
Ferdinand *King of* Spain,	Mr. *Littlewood.*
Duke of Arcos,	Mr. *Bell.*

[15]

Women.

Almahide, *Queen of*	Mrs. *Ellen Gwin.*
Granada,	

---

[85] Dryden's two-part play received its première in December 1670 and January 1671. Downes' cast was for the first production and remained available only until Nell Gwyn left the stage in the spring of 1671. The edition of 1672 confirms Downes' cast and adds: Zulema—[William] Harris; Selin—Wintershall; Ozmyn—[George?] Beeston; Hamet—Watson; Gomel—Powell; Halyma—Mrs. Eastland.

Lindaraxa,	Mrs. *Marshall*.
Benzaida,	Mrs. *Boutell*.
Esperanza,	Mrs. *Reeves*.
Isabella *Queen of* Spain,	Mrs. *James*.

Sophonisba, or Hanibal's Overthrow.[86]

Hannibal,	Major *Mohun*.
Maherbal,	Mr. *Burt*.
Bomilcar,	Mr. *Wintersel*.
Scipio,	Mr. *Kynaston*.
Lelius,	Mr. *Lydall*.
Massinissa,	Mr. *Hart*.
Massina,	Mr. *Clark*.

Women.

---

[86] Lee's tragedy received its première in April 1675. Although Downes' cast was probably not that of the first production, everyone he names would have been available from the time of the première to ca. 1677-78 (when Lydall and William Harris evidently left the company) or Burt's retirement from performance in 1678. On the complexities presented by this cast, see Endnote 2.

Sophonisba,	Mrs. *Cox*.
Rosalinda,	Mrs. *Boutel*.[87]

Note, All the foregoing, both Old and Modern Plays being the Principal in their Stock and most taking, yet, they Acted divers others, which to Enumerate in order, wou'd tire the Patience of the Reader. As[88] *Country Wife*; *Love in a Wood*; *St. James's-Park*;[89] *Amboina*; *The Cheats*; *Selindra*; *The Surprizal*; *Vestal Virgin*; *The Committee*; *Love in a Maze*; *The Rehearsal*: In which last, Mr. *Lacy*,[90]

[16]

For his Just Acting, all gave him due Praise,
His Part in the Cheats, Jony Thump, Teg *and* Bayes,
In these Four Excelling; The Court gave him the Bays.

And many others were Acted by the Old Company at the Theatre Royal, from the time they begun, till the Patent descended to

---

[87] Listed as Mrs. Damport in Q1.

[88] Wycherley, *The Country-Wife* (acted by 12 January 1675), and *Love in a Wood* (ca. March 1671); Dryden, *Amboyna* (ca. May? 1672); Wilson, *The Cheats* (March 1663); Sir William Killigrew, *Selindra* (3 March 1662); Sir Robert Howard, *The Surprisal* (April 1662), *The Vestal-Virgin* (ca. October 1664?), and *The Committee* (November 1662); James Shirley, *Love in a Maze* [*The Changes*] (by 17 May 1662); Buckingham, *The Rehearsal* (early December 1671).

[89] Alternative title for Wycherley's *Love in a Wood*, just preceding in this list.

[90] John Lacy played Scruple in Wilson's *The Cheats* (March 1663), Jonny Thump in Shirley's *The Changes* (May 1662), Teague in Howard's *The Committee* (November 1662), and Bayes in Buckingham's *The Rehearsal* (December 1671). Langbaine comments: "as I remember, the deceas'd Mr. *Lacy* acted *Jonny Thump*, Sir *Gervase Simple*'s Man, with general Applause" (p. 477).

Mr. *Charles Killigrew*,[91] which in 1682, he join'd it to Dr. *Davenant*'s Patent,[92] whose Company Acted then in *Dorset* Garden, which upon the Union, were Created the King's Company:[93] After which, Mr. *Hart* Acted no more, having a Pension to the Day of his Death, from the United Company.[94]

I must not Omit to mention the Parts in several Plays of some of the Actors; wherein they Excell'd in the Performance of them. *First*, Mr. *Hart*, in the Part of *Arbaces*, in *King and no King*; *Amintor*, in the *Maids Tragedy*; *Othello*; *Rollo*; *Brutus*, in *Julius Cæsar*; *Alexander*,[95] towards the latter End of his Acting; if he Acted in any one of these but once in a Fortnight, the House was fill'd as at a New Play, especially *Alexander*, he Acting that with such Grandeur and Agreeable Majesty, That one of the Court was pleas'd to Honour him with this Commendation; That *Hart* might Teach any King on Earth how to Comport himself: He was no less Inferior[96] in Comedy; as *Mosca* in the *Fox*; *Don John* in the *Chances*, *Wildblood* in the *Mock Astrologer*; with sundry other Parts. In all the Comedies and Tragedies, he was concern'd he Perform'd with that Exactness and Perfection, that not any of his Successors have Equall'd him.

---

[91] Thomas Killigrew did not die until 1683, but his son Charles took control in February 1677 after an extended period of bickering within the company. See particularly P.R.O. C6/221/48 (Charles Killigrew vs. Thomas Killigrew, et al.) and LC 5/141, p. 539 (the Lord Chamberlain's order of 22 February 1676/7, giving control to Charles Killigrew). For discussion, see Hotson, Chapter 6.

[92] See note 110, below.

[93] The members of the company created by the joining of the two patents became "Their Majesties Servants." The resultant company is almost always termed the United Company by modern scholars, until the split caused by the actor rebellion of 1694-95, after which it is generally called the Patent Company. These were not, however, official, advertised names.

[94] Downes comments further about Hart's pension on page 81, below.

[95] In Lee's *The Rival Queens* (March 1677).

[96] I.e., not inferior. Hart was equally good in tragedy and in comedy.

[17]

Major *Mohun*, he was Eminent for *Volpone*; *Face* in the *Alchymist*; *Melantius* in the *Maids Tragedy*; *Mardonius*, in *King and no King*; *Cassius*, in *Julius Cæsar*; *Clytus*, in *Alexander*; *Mithridates*, &c. An Eminent Poet[97] seeing him Act this last, vented suddenly this Saying; Oh *Mohun, Mohun! Thou little Man of Mettle, if I should Write a 100 Plays, I'd Write a Part for thy Mouth*; in short, in all his Parts, he was most Accurate and Correct.

Mr. *Wintersel*, was good in Tragedy, as well as in Comedy, especially in Cokes in *Bartholomew-Fair*; that the Famous Comedian *Nokes* came in that part far short of him.

Then Mr. *Burt, Shatterel, Cartwright* and several other good Actors, but to Particularize their Commendations wou'd be too Tedious; I refer you therefore to the several Books, their Names being there inserted.[98]

Next follows an Account of the Rise and Progression, of the Dukes Servants; under the Patent of Sir *William Davenant* who upon the said Junction in 1682, remov'd to the Theatre Royal in *Drury-Lane*,[99] and Created the King's Company.

---

[97] From the context, probably the author of *Mithridates* (1678), Nathaniel Lee.

[98] I.e., to play quartos, in many of which the actors' names were printed in the Dramatis Personae lists.

[99] At the time of the Union of 1682 the United Company managers agreed to pay rent on both the Dorset Garden and Drury Lane theatres every acting day, regardless of which building was used. The daily rent on Dorset Garden was £7, and a reduction was negotiated in the Drury Lane rent from £5 14s to £3 (see British Library Add. Charter 9298, and Hotson, p. 283). Downes is incorrect in saying that the joint company simply moved to Drury Lane: both theatres continued in regular use into the 1690s. Dorset Garden was definitely used for operas and plays demanding fancy staging; how much it was used for regular plays we do not know. For a consideration of the problem, see Robert D. Hume, "The Nature of the Dorset Garden Theatre," *Theatre Notebook*, 36 (1982), 99-109.

In the Year 1659,[100] General *Monk*, Marching then his Army
out of *Scotland* to *London*. Mr. *Rhodes* a Bookseller being Ward-
robe-Keeper formerly (as I am inform'd) to King *Charles* the First's,
Company of Comedians in *Black-Friars*;[101] getting a License from
the then Governing State, fitted up a House then for Acting call'd
the *Cock-Pit* in *Drury-Lane*, and in a short time Compleated his
Company.[102]

[18]

Their Names were, *viz.*[103]

---

[100] Downes almost certainly means 1659/60. See Endnote 3.

[101] This is possible but unconfirmed. A plenitude of references to "John
Rhodes" between 1624 and 1660 leads Bentley (II, 544-546) to hypothesize
the existence of three separate people with this name. Whether the same
John Rhodes was both a bookseller and the one-time Wardrobe Keeper to
the pre-war King's Company we cannot be certain.

[102] On the complex maneuvering and infighting that led to the creation
of the patent monopoly, see particularly John Freehafer, "The Formation
of the London Patent Companies in 1660," *Theatre Notebook*, 20 (1965),
6-30, and Gunnar Sorelius, "The Early History of the Restoration Theatre:
Some Problems Reconsidered," *Theatre Notebook*, 33 (1979), 52-61.

[103] Downes is our only definite source for the members of Rhodes' company. All of the actors in the left-hand list save James Dixon signed the
Duke's Company sharing agreement of 5 November 1660 (British Library
Add. Charter 9295, printed in Herbert, *Dramatic Records*, pp. 96-100,
from Malone and Halliwell-Phillipps' transcriptions of British Library Add.
MS 19,256, fols. 53-60). Independent confirmation of Dixon's presence in
the company is provided by his inclusion in a list of actors fined for
assaulting a messenger from the Office of the Revels on 4 July 1662 (see
Hotson, p. 212).

Mr. *Betterton.*	*Note*, These six commonly
Mr. *Sheppy.*	Acted Womens Parts.
Mr. *Lovel.*	Mr. *Kynaston.*
Mr. *Lilliston.*	*James Nokes.*
Mr. *Underhill.*	Mr. *Angel.*
Mr. *Turner.*	*William Betterton.*
Mr. *Dixon.*	Mr. *Mosely.*
Robert Nokes.	Mr. *Floid.*

The Plays there Acted were,[104]

The Loyal Subject.
Maid in the Mill.
The Wild Goose Chase.
The Spanish Curate.
The Mad Lover.
Pericles, Prince of Tyre.

---

[104] Except for the following, these plays are part of the 'Fletcher' canon. *Pericles* (ca. 1608) is by Shakespeare; *The Unfortunate Lovers* (1638) is by Davenant; *Aglaura* (1637) is by Suckling; *The Changeling* (1622) is by Middleton and Rowley; *The Bondman* (1623) is by Massinger. This list is the principal evidence for Rhodes' repertory. Pepys saw Kynaston as the Duke's sister in Fletcher's *Loyal Subject* at the Cockpit on 18 August 1660. In his 1710 *Life of Betterton* (p. 5), Charles Gildon states that Betterton "got a great Applause" in *The Loyal Subject, The Wild Goose Chase, The Spanish Curate,* "and many more"—a statement that may, of course, be extrapolated from Downes. On Gildon's authority, see p. 109, n. 398, below.

A Wife for a Month.
Rule Wife and have a Wife.
The Tamer Tam'd.
The Unfortunate Lovers.
Aglaura.
Changling.
Bondman. With divers others.

Mr. *Betterton*, being then but 22 Years Old,[105] was highly Applauded for his Acting in all these Plays, but especially, For the *Loyal Subject*; *The Mad Lover*; *Pericles*; *The Bondman*: *Deflores*, in the *Changling*; his Voice being then as Audibly strong, full and Articulate, as in the Prime of his Acting.

[19]

Mr. *Sheppy*[106] Perform'd *Theodore* in the *Loyal Subject*; Duke *Altophil*, in the *Unfortunate Lovers*; *Asotus*, in the *Bondman*, and several other Parts very well; But above all the *Changling*, with general Satisfaction.

Mr. *Kynaston*[107] Acted *Arthiope*, in the *Unfortunate Lovers*; The Princess in the *Mad Lover*; *Aglaura*; *Ismenia*, in the *Maid in the*

---

[105] Thomas Betterton (1635-1710) can be documented from October 1660 to his death in April 1710. Downes is the principal evidence for his having acted with Rhodes, which he did at the age of 24, not 22.

[106] Downes is our only evidence for Thomas Sheppey's beginning with Rhodes. He signed the Duke's Company articles in November 1660, but no roles for him are known after 1661. In 1673 he invested in Drury Lane, and by 1675 he was formally a member of the King's Company, though perhaps only in a managerial capacity (Hotson, p. 254, and P.R.O. LC 3/28, pp. 201-202).

[107] Pepys' diary for 18 August 1660 confirms Downes' statement that Edward Kynaston (1643-1712) acted women's roles at the Cockpit. However, Kynaston joined the King's Company in the autumn of 1660, not the Duke's. He later made a place for himself in the United Company, and his career lasted until about 1701. We do not know who succeeded Kynaston in the roles of Arthiope and Aglaura.

Mill; and several other Womens Parts; he being then very Young made a Compleat Female Stage Beauty, performing his Parts so well, especially *Arthiope* and *Aglaura*, being Parts greatly moving Compassion and Pity; that it has since been Disputable among the Judicious, whether any Woman that succeeded him so Sensibly touch'd the Audience as he.

Mr. *James Nokes*[108] Acted first, *The Maid in the Mill*; after him Mr. *Angel*;[109] *Aminta* in the same Play was Acted by Mr. *William Betterton* (who not long after was Drown'd in Swimming at *Wallingford*). They Acted several other Womens Parts in the said Plays, very Acceptable to the Audience: *Mosely* and *Floid* commonly Acted the Part of a Bawd and Whore.

In this Interim, Sir *William Davenant* gain'd a Patent from the King,[110] and Created Mr. *Betterton* and all the Rest[111] of *Rhodes's*

---

[108] Downes is our only evidence that James Nokes (*d.* 1696) began as a boy-actor, an assertion that makes sense in light of the late date he was "sworn," 13 January 1667[/8?]—(LC 3/25, p. 162). He made the transition to male roles successfully but also played travesty parts that earned him the nickname "Nurse."

[109] Apart from Downes' testimony, little is known of Angel (*d.* 1673?), Moseley, Floyd, or William Betterton (1644-1661). On Angel, see "An Elegy Upon that Incomparable *Comedian*, Mr. Edward Angell" (1673?), not in Arnott and Robinson, but reprinted from a broadside copy in *A Little Ark*, ed. G. Thorn-Drury, pp. 38-39.

[110] The patent was formally issued on 15 January 1662/3. The official roll-copy is now P.R.O. C66/3009, no. 3; what was evidently Davenant's exemplification is now in the Philip H. and A. S. W. Rosenbach Foundation Museum, Philadelphia. The text is printed complete by Fitzgerald, I, 73-77, and by Geoffrey Ashton and Iain Mackintosh in *Royal Opera House Retrospective 1732-1982* [exhibition catalogue] (London: Royal Academy, 1982), pp. 20-22, with a photographic reproduction of the Rosenbach copy.

[111] Except for Edward Kynaston, all of the actors Downes names for Rhodes' Company are known to have joined the Duke's Company. All but Angel, Dixon, William Betterton, Moseley, and Floyd are confirmed by other sources for the season of 1660-61.

Company, the King's Servants;[112] who were Sworn by my Lord *Manchester* then Lord Chamberlain, to Serve his Royal Highness the Duke of *York*, at the Theatre in *Lincoln's-Inn Fields*.

Note, The four following, were new Actors taken in by Sir *William*, to Compleat[113] the Company he had from Mr. *Rhodes*.

[20]

Mr. *Harris*.[114]   Mr. *Richards*.[115]

---

[112] Accurate, but puzzling. In LC 3/25, p. 162 is a list headed "Sir William Davenants Comœdians sworne to attend his Royall Highnesse the Duke of Yorke." "Richard" Sandford, Robert Noakes, Richard Badeley, William Cory, and Joseph Price were sworn on 24 September 1662. Some thirteen others were sworn at various times during the next six years. This list was copied (ca. 1670?) and continued in LC 3/26, p. 210. For synoptic summaries of such rosters, see John Harold Wilson, "Players' Lists in the Lord Chamberlain's *Registers*," *Theatre Notebook*, 18 (1963), 25-30. A number of major actors and all Duke's Company women are missing from these records, but petitions to the Lord Chamberlain requesting permission to sue actors prove that the Duke's Company personnel enjoyed the protected legal status of King's servants.

[113] Here and on page 50 Downes uses the term "Compleat" to refer to changes that occurred over a period of several years.

[114] Henry Harris (ca. 1634-1704) joined Davenant's company 5 November 1660, serving as a principal actor and later as co-manager until about 1677. He became Yeoman of the Revels in 1663 and retired completely from acting in 1681.

[115] We do not know exactly when John Richards (1629?-1688?) joined the company. Downes lists him for various early casts. On 6 August 1662 Lord Chamberlain Manchester complained to the Irish authorities that Ogilby had enticed Richards to Dublin and asked that he be compelled to return (P.R.O. SP 29/58, no. 15I). There is no definite evidence that he did so until 1676, after which he performed regularly until he went back to Dublin ca. 1683-84. All roles assigned to Richards in *The London Stage* between spring 1662 and 1676 must be viewed with skepticism, at least as

Mr. *Price.*[116] | Mr. *Blagden.*[117]

The Five following came not in till almost a Year after they begun.

Mr. *Smith.*[118] | Mr. *Young.*[119]

---

regards the dating.

[116] Joseph Price remains a shadowy figure. He was sworn a comedian on 24 September 1662 (LC 3/25, p. 162); we do not know when he joined. There is no record of him in London after 1664-65 except for his inclusion as Malateste in a problematical cast given in the 1678 edition of *The Duchess of Malfi*, a cast that includes Price and Richards but otherwise points to performance ca. 1672 or spring 1673. The *Biographical Dictionary* mentions traces of a Price in Dublin. Downes implies on page 74 that Price died ca. 1673-74, but this date cannot be accepted with any confidence.

[117] This entry is consistent with Blagden's presence in the cast Downes gives for *The Siege of Rhodes* in June 1661. He transferred to the King's Company for the season of 1661-62 and remained there.

[118] William Smith's first definite role was the young lover in a performance of *Ignoramus* at court in November 1662. He became a mainstay of the Duke's and United Companies, serving as co-manager with Betterton from 1677 to the autumn of 1687. He came out of retirement to join the Lincoln's Inn Fields company in 1695 but died in December (see page 92, below).

[119] John Young's first known role (on Downes' word) was in *The Villain*, early in the 1662-63 season. He was not sworn until 13 January 1667[/8?]. He seems not to have been a principal actor, though at least once he deputized for Betterton during Betterton's illness in 1667-68. His last certain role is in *The Fatal Jealousie* in August 1672. Young was financially irresponsible, and the Lord Chamberlain's records show that he was heavily in debt by September 1672. He may well have fled his creditors at that time.

Mr. *Sandford.*[120]   Mr. *Norris.*[121]

Mr. *Medburn.*[122]

Sir *William Davenant*'s Women Actresses were,[123]

Note, These Four being his Principal Actresses, he Boarded them at his own House.

Mrs. *Davenport.*[124]   Mrs. *Davies.*[125]

---

[120] If Downes' cast for *Cutter of Coleman-Street* reflects the original production, Samuel Sandford was performing important roles by 16 December 1661. He was one of the actors who beat up a messenger from the Revels Office on 4 July 1662 (*Middlesex County Records*, Vol. III, ed. John Cordy Jeaffreson [London, 1888], pp. 322-323). He continued to play character parts until about 1698; he was especially noted for his villains (see page 54, below).

[121] Henry Norris the elder is listed in the *Ignoramus* cast for 1 November 1662. He may not have returned to the company immediately after the plague. He was sworn a comedian on 7 August 1669, after which he continued to play small roles through 1687.

[122] Matthew Medbourne was involved in the attack on a Revels Office messenger, 4 July 1662. He was arrested in the early days of the Popish Plot scare in 1678 and died in prison in 1680.

[123] We have no way to tell when each of these women joined the company. No women appear in the first Duke's Company list of "sworn comedians" (LC 3/25, p. 162).

[124] Hester Davenport's first known role was Roxolana in *The Siege of Rhodes* (June 1661). According to Pepys, she had left the stage by 18 February 1662. She may have returned briefly a year later; see pages 53-54, below. She was not related to the Davenport sisters who worked for the King's Company.

[125] Mary (or Moll) Davis was seen for the first time by Pepys on 18 February 1662, who called her "the little girl." She acted numerous roles prior to her departure from the stage in May 1668 to become mistress to

Mrs. *Saunderson.*[126]   Mrs. *Long.*[127]

Mrs. *Ann Gibbs.*[128]   Mrs. *Holden.*[129]

Mrs. *Norris.*[130]   Mrs. *Jennings.*[131]

His Company being now Compleat, Sir *William* in order to pre-
pare Plays to Open his Theatre, it being then a Building in *Lincoln's-Inn Fields*, His Company Rehears'd the First and Second Part
of the *Siege of Rhodes*; and the *Wits* at *Pothecaries-Hall*:[132] And in

---

Charles II.

[126] Mary Saunderson's first known role was Ianthe in *The Siege of
Rhodes* (June 1661)—assuming that Downes' cast was for the original pro-
duction. The license for her marriage to Thomas Betterton is dated 24
December 1662. She continued to act until about 1694.

[127] If Downes' cast reflects the first production, Jane Long's first known
role is in *Cutter of Coleman-Street* (December 1661). She left the stage in
1673 to become the mistress of George Porter.

[128] Anne Gibbs' first definite London role is in *Cutter of Coleman-Street*
in December 1661—assuming that Downes gives us the cast for the first
production. She married Thomas Shadwell ca. 1664 but acted (with inter-
ruptions) until 1681.

[129] Aside from this entry and Downes' anecdote about *Romeo and Juliet*
on page 53, we have no record of Mrs. Holden.

[130] Mrs. [Henry?] Norris' first definite role is in *Ignoramus* (1 November
1662). She played a long succession of small character parts until about
1683.

[131] Mrs. Jennings' first certain role is in *Ignoramus* (1 November 1662).
Her last definite appearance is in *Cambyses* in January 1671. Downes
includes her in his list of actresses "by force of Love . . . Erept the Stage"
(p. 74).

[132] Summers (pp. 176-177) points out that there is ballad evidence that
Davenant used this building in 1656.

Spring 1662,[133] Open'd his House with the said Plays, having new Scenes and Decorations, being the first that e're were Introduc'd in *England*.[134] Mr. *Betterton*, Acted Soly-man the Magnificent; Mr. *Harris*, *Alphonso*; Mr. *Lilliston*, *Villerius* the Grand Master; Mr. *Blagden* the Admiral; Mrs. *Davenport*, *Roxolana*; Mrs. *Sanderson* Ianthe:[135]

[21]

All Parts being Justly and Excellently Perform'd; it continu'd Acting 12 Days without Interruption with great Applause.

The next was the *Wits*,[136] a Comedy, Writ by Sir *William Davenant*; The Part of the Elder *Palatine*, Perform'd by Mr. *Betterton*; The Younger *Palatine* by Mr. *Harris*, Sir *Morgly Thwack*, by Mr. *Underhill*; Lady *Ample*, by Mrs. *Davenport*: All the other Parts being exactly Perform'd; it continu'd 8 Days Acting Successively.

The Tragedy of *Hamlet*;[137] *Hamlet* being Perform'd by Mr. *Betterton*, Sir *William* (having seen Mr. *Taylor* of the *Black-Fryars* Company Act it, who being Instructed by the Author Mr. *Shakespear*)[138]

---

[133] *Recte* June 1661. Pepys saw the second part of *The Siege of Rhodes* on 2 July 1661, specifying that this was "the fourth day" the theatre was open.

[134] I.e., Lincoln's Inn Fields was the first public theatre in England to have changeable scenery. Summers cites *Historia Histrionica* (1699) as evidence of this assertion (p. 177).

[135] Q1663 gives no actors' names.

[136] Pepys saw Davenant's play (1634) newly staged with scenery on 15 August 1661. His comment implies that it had been in the repertory at Salisbury Court that spring. Downes is our only source for the cast.

[137] Pepys saw *Hamlet* on 24 August 1661, though that was not necessarily the first performance. He confirms Betterton as Hamlet on this day. The presence of Richards and Mrs. Davenport implies a date of 1661 or very early 1662 for this cast. Dacres does not help with the date, since Downes is our only source for him. We have no other cast for *Hamlet* until Q1676, which lists the actors for a production in the early seventies.

[138] Bentley points out that both Shakespeare and Burbage, who first played Hamlet, were dead before Joseph Taylor joined the King's Men in

taught Mr. *Betterton* in every Particle of it; which by his exact Performance of it, gain'd him Esteem and Reputation, Superlative to all other Plays. *Horatio* by Mr. *Harris*; The King by Mr. *Lilliston*; The Ghost by Mr. *Richards*, (after by Mr. *Medburn*); *Polonius* by Mr. *Lovel*; *Rosencrans* by Mr. *Dixon*; *Guilderstern* by Mr. *Price*; 1st, Grave-maker, by Mr. *Underhill*: The 2d, by Mr. *Dacres*; The Queen, by Mrs. *Davenport*; *Ophelia*, by Mrs. *Sanderson*: No succeeding Tragedy for several Years got more Reputation, or Money to the Company than this.

 Love and Honour,[139] wrote by Sir *William Davenant*: This Play was Richly Cloath'd;[140] The King giving Mr. *Betterton* his Coronation Suit, in which, he Acted the Part of Prince *Alvaro*; The Duke of *York* giving Mr. *Harris* his, who did Prince *Prospero*; And my Lord of *Oxford*, gave Mr. *Joseph Price* his, who did *Lionel*

[22]

the Duke of *Parma*'s Son; The Duke was Acted by Mr. *Lilliston*; *Evandra*, by Mrs. *Davenport*, and all the other Parts being very well done: The Play having a great run, Produc'd to the Company great Gain and Estimation from the Town.

 Romeo and Juliet,[141] Wrote by Mr. *Shakespear*: *Romeo*, was Acted by Mr. *Harris*; *Mercutio*, by Mr. *Betterton*; Count *Paris*, by

---

1619 (II, 597). This tale seems of a piece with Davenant's sometime claim to be Shakespeare's illegitimate son, but however spurious the interpretation of the role, the anecdote indicates respect for a performance tradition. Compare page 55, below.

[139] Pepys attended the première, 21 October 1661. Other sources confirm that all the actors Downes reports were available at that time.

[140] For the Duke's Company to get the Coronation suits suggests imaginative and aggressive lobbying on Davenant's part. Downes tells a similar story about Orrery's *Henry the Fifth* in 1664 (see p. 61, below). The suits were evidently borrowed, returned, and borrowed again, not given to the company.

[141] Pepys records what he says was the first performance (i.e., since the Restoration), 1 March 1662. All of Downes' cast was presumably available, though we have no other record of Mrs. Holden.

Mr. *Price*; The *Fryar*, by Mr. *Richards*; *Sampson*, by Mr. *Sandford*; *Gregory*, by Mr. *Underhill*; *Juliet*, by Mrs. *Saunderson*; Count *Paris*'s Wife, by Mrs. *Holden*.

Note, There being a Fight and Scuffle in this Play, between the House of *Capulet*, and House of *Paris*; Mrs. *Holden* Acting his Wife, enter'd in a *Hurry*, Crying, O my Dear *Count*! She Inadvertently left out, O, in the pronuntiation of the Word *Count*! giving it a Vehement Accent, put the House into such a Laughter, that *London* Bridge at low Water was silence to it.[142]

This Tragedy of *Romeo and Juliet*, was made some time after into a Tragi-comedy, by Mr. *James Howard*,[143] he preserving *Romeo* and *Juliet* alive; so that when the Tragedy was Reviv'd again, 'twas Play'd Alternately, Tragical one Day, and Tragicomical another; for several Days together.

The Adventures of five Hours, Wrote by the Earl of *Bristol*, and Sir *Samuel Tuke*:[144] This Play being Cloath'd so Excellently Fine in proper Habits, and Acted so justly well. Mr. *Betterton*, Acting *Don*

---

[142] Waldron (1789, p. 31) goes to some lengths to try to cast doubt on the authenticity of "this silly and indecent passage," objecting that there is no "House of Paris" in Shakespeare's play. Why he asserts that Howard's tragicomic version "could not . . . be the Piece in the representation of which the accident happened" we do not see. As late as 1927 Hazelton Spencer still considered the passage "unprintable" (*Shakespeare Improved* [1927; rpt. New York: Ungar, 1963], p. 73). For a speculative argument that Shakespeare's play was altered even before Howard reworked it, see Christopher Spencer, "'Count Paris's Wife': *Romeo and Juliet* on the Early Restoration Stage," *Texas Studies in Language and Literature*, 7 (1965-66), 309-316.

[143] On this adaptation, see "Lost English Plays," no. 15. James Howard's other playwriting all precedes the closing of the theatres on account of plague in June 1665, so probably this adaptation does too.

[144] Pepys attended the première, 8 January 1663. Bristol did write "Spanish romances," but all other sources suggest that Tuke was sole author of this play. The edition of 1663 gives no actors' names. The only difficulty raised by Downes' cast is with Mrs. Davenport. Assuming that this is Hester Davenport, she must have made an otherwise unrecorded return to the stage at this time.

Henriq; Mr. *Harris, Antonio*; Mr. *Young, Octavio*; Mr. *Underhill, Diego*; Mr. *Sandford, Ernesto*; Mr. *Smith*, the *Corrigidor*; Mr. *Price, Silvio*; Mrs. *Davenport, Camilla*; Mrs.

[23]

Betterton, Portia; Mrs. *Long, Flora*. It took Successively 13 Days together, no other Play Intervening.

Twelfth Night, Or what you will;[145] Wrote by Mr. *Shakespear*, had mighty Success by its well Performance: Sir *Toby Belch*, by Mr. *Betterton*; Sir *Andrew Ague-Cheek*, by Mr. *Harris*; *Fool*, by Mr. *Underhill*; *Malvolio* the Steward, by Mr. *Lovel*; *Olivia*, by Mrs. *Ann Gibbs*; All the Parts being justly Acted Crown'd the Play. *Note*, It was got up on purpose to be Acted on Twelfth Night.

The Villain,[146] Written by Major *Thomas Porter*; this Play by its being well perform'd, had Success extremly beyond the Company's Expectation. Mr. *Betterton*, Acting *Monsieur Brisac*, Mr. *Harris, Monsieur Beaupre*; Governour, Mr. *Lilliston*; *Boutefeu*, Mr. *Young. Maligni*, the Villain, Mr. *Saunford*;[147] *Coligni*, the Scriveners Son, by that Inimitable Sprightly Actor, Mr. *Price*; (especially in this part); *Bellmont*, by Mrs. *Betterton*: It Succeeded 10 Days with a full House, to the last.

---

[145] Pepys calls this "a new play" on 11 September 1661, which is odd if Downes is correct that "It was got up on purpose to be Acted on Twelfth Night." If Pepys is right, then the holiday performance must have come in 1662 or later. Alternatively, we may wonder if Davenant opened at Salisbury Court in January 1661 with this play. Downes' cast is possible for September 1661. Anne Gibbs worked with the Red Bull Company in Oxford in July but could have joined the Duke's Company any time thereafter. See Sybil Rosenfeld, "Some Notes on the Players in Oxford, 1661-1713," *Review of English Studies*, 19 (1943), 366-375.

[146] Pepys says that this play was first performed on 18 October 1662. The edition of 1663 gives no actors' names. This cast is our earliest record of Young, but the others were all available.

[147] Samuel Sandford became famous for this role. See Robert H. Ross, Jr., "Samuel Sandford: Villain from Necessity," *PMLA*, 76 (1961), 367-372.

The Rivals,[148] A Play, Wrote by Sir *William Davenant*; having a very Fine Interlude in it, of Vocal and Instrumental Musick, mixt with very Diverting Dances; Mr. *Price* introducing the Dancing, by a short Comical Prologue, gain'd him an Universal Applause of the Town. The Part of *Theocles*, was done by Mr. *Harris*; *Philander*, by Mr. *Betterton*; *Cunopes* the Jailor, by Mr. *Underhill*: And all the Womens Parts admirably Acted; chiefly *Celia*, a Sheperdess being Mad for Love; especially in Singing several Wild and Mad Songs.

[24]

My Lodging it is on the Cold Ground, &c. She perform'd that so Charmingly, that not long after, it Rais'd her from her Bed on the Cold Ground, to a Bed Royal.[149] The Play by the Excellent performance; lasted uninterruptly Nine Days, with a full Audience.

King Henry the 8th,[150] This Play, by Order of Sir *William Davenant*, was all new Cloath'd in proper Habits: The King's was new, all the Lords, the Cardinals, the Bishops, the Doctors, Proctors, Lawyers, Tip-staves, new Scenes: The part of the King was so right and justly done by Mr. *Betterton*, he being Instructed in it by Sir *William*, who had it from Old Mr. *Lowen*, that had his Instructions from Mr. *Shakespear* himself,[151] that I dare and will aver, none

---

[148] Pepys saw this play on 10 September 1664 but does not say that it was new. Downes' cast would all have been available then or in the previous season. Q1668 adds: Arcon—Young; Polynices—Smith; Provost—Sandford; Heraclia—Mrs. Shadwell; Leucippe—Mrs. Long. Pepys implies that Winifred Gosnell took the part Downes calls "Celia" (i.e., Celania), for which Q1668 gives Mrs. Davis. Mary Davis evidently succeeded Gosnell (who "fell out of the key" the day Pepys saw her in the role).

[149] On Mary Davis and her brief period as a mistress of Charles II, which began in the winter of 1667-68, see *Biographical Dictionary*, IV, 222-226. The King definitely saw a performance of *The Rivals* on 19 November 1667 (LC list).

[150] On 10 December 1663 Pepys reported that this play was supposed to open "this week." Downes is the only source for the cast.

[151] On John Lowin (1576-1653), see Bentley, II, 499-506. This tradition is possible, unlike the one about Taylor (see pp. 51-52, above).

can, or will come near him in this Age, in the performance of that part: Mr. *Harris*'s, performance of Cardinal *Wolsey*, was little Inferior to that, he doing it with such just State, Port and Mein, that I dare affirm, none hitherto has Equall'd him:[152] The Duke of *Buckingham*, by Mr. *Smith*; *Norfolk*, by Mr. *Nokes*; *Suffolk*, by Mr. *Lilliston*; Cardinal *Campeius* and *Cranmur*, by Mr. *Medburn*; Bishop *Gardiner*, by Mr. *Underhill*; Earl of *Surry*, by Mr. *Young*; Lord *Sands*, by Mr. *Price*; Mrs. *Betterton*, Queen *Catherine*: Every part by the great Care of Sir *William*, being exactly perform'd; it being all new Cloath'd and new Scenes; it continu'd Acting 15 Days together with general Applause.

Love in a Tub,[153] Wrote by Sir *George Etheridge*; Mr. *Betterton*, performing Lord *Beauford*; Mr. *Smith*, Colonel *Bruce*; Mr. *Norris*, *Lovis*; Mr. *Nokes*, Sir *Nicholas Cully*; Mr. *Underhill*, *Palmer*;

[25]

Mr. *Saunford*, Wheadle; Mrs. *Betterton*, *Graciana*; Mrs. *Davies*, *Aurelia*; Mrs. *Long*, the Widow; Mr. *Harris*, Sir *Frederick Frollick*; Mr. *Price*, *Dufoy*.[154]

> *Sir* Nich'las, *Sir* Fred'rick; *Widow and* Dufoy,
> *Were not by any so well done*, Mafoy:

---

[152] We do not know who succeeded Harris as Wolsey. Underhill is the only actor tentatively recorded for the Lincoln's Inn Fields performance in November 1700, but when Betterton took Henry VIII at the Haymarket in February 1707 Verbruggen played Wolsey. We have no cast for the Drury Lane production of March 1708, other than Betterton as the King.

[153] The first recorded performance of *The Comical Revenge, or Love in a Tub* is 27 April 1664, from which the *London Stage* editors conjecture a première in March, though mid-April seems more likely to us in view of known performances of other plays. Downes is the only source for the cast, which poses no problems.

[154] Our next full cast for this play is not until 14 December 1706 when Norris played Sir Nicholas; Wilks, Sir Frederick; Mrs. Oldfield, the Widow; and Bowen, Dufoy. Doggett was probably a fine Sir Nicholas (10 January 1705).

The clean and well performance of this Comedy, got the Company more Reputation and Profit than any preceding Comedy; the Company taking in a Months time at it 1000*l.*[155]

Cutter of Coleman-street;[156] Written by Mr. *Abraham Cowley*; Colonel *Jolly*, perform'd by Mr. *Betterton*; Old *True-man*, by Mr. *Lovel*; Young *True-man*, Mr. *Harris*; *Cutter*, Mr. *Underhill*; Captain *Worme*, Mr. *Sandford*; Parson *Soaker*, Mr. *Dacres*; *Puny*, Mr. *Nokes*; *Will*, Mr. *Price*; *Aurelia*, by Mrs. *Betterton*; *Lucia*, Mrs. *Ann Gibbs*; Laughing *Jane*, by Mrs. *Long*: This Comedy being Acted so perfectly Well and Exact, it was perform'd a whole Week with a full Audience.

Note, This Play was not a little injurious to the Cavalier Indigent Officers; especially the Character of *Cutter* and *Worm*.[157]

The Dutchess of Malfey;[158] Wrote by Mr. *Webster*: Duke

---

[155] Downes presumably means net profit, which would imply (for example) fifteen performances in a month at an average gross of about £90 per day. House charges were approximately £25 at this time. If Downes means gross, then only £66 per day would be required, and the net would have been about £600.

[156] Cowley's play was written in 1642 (as *The Guardian*) and revised in 1661. Pepys attended the première on 16 December 1661. Downes is our only source for the cast, which presents no problems. Cowley describes Cutter as "A merry sharking fellow about the Town, pretending to have been a Colonel in the Kings Army" and Worm as "His Companion, and such another fellow, pretending to have been a Captain." Cowley's defensive preface to the edition of 1663 shows that the audience took offense at his treatment of the pseudo-royalist "officers."

[157] This sentence was printed in small type to the right of the *Cutter* paragraph in the edition of 1708.

[158] The first recorded performance after the Restoration is from Pepys, 30 September 1662. All of Downes' cast would have been available then. The earliest published cast (a composite from different productions?) appeared in the 1678 quarto, from which *The London Stage* adds to the 1662 cast the following actors: Delio—Medbourne; Castruchio—Richards [in Dublin in September 1662]; Sylvio—Cademan; Pescara—Norris; Malateste—Price; Cariola—Mrs. Norris.

Ferdinand, Perform'd by Mr. *Harris*: *Bosola*, by Mr. *Betterton*:
Antonio, Mr. *Smith*: *Cardinal*, Mr. *Young*: Dutchess of *Malfey*, by
Mrs. *Betterton*: *Julia*, the *Cardinals* Mistress, by Mrs. *Gibbs*: This
Play was so exceeding Excellently Acted in all Parts; chiefly, Duke
Ferdinand and *Bosola*: It fill'd the House 8 Days Successively, it
proving one of the Best of Stock Tragedies.

The Tragedy of Mustapha,[159] Wrote by the Earl of *Orrery*. The
part of *Solyman* the Magnificent,

[26]

was done by Mr. *Betterton*: *Mustapha*, Mr. *Harris*: *Zanger*, Mr.
Smith: *Rustan*, Mr. *Sandford*: *Pyrrhus*, Mr. *Richards*: Cardinal of
Veradium,[160] Mr. *Young*: *Haly*, Mr. *Cademan*: *Roxolana*, Mrs.
Davenport: (Afterward[161] Mrs. *Betterton*, and then by one Mrs.
Wiseman):[162] Queen of *Hungaria*, Mrs. *Davies*. All the Parts being
new Cloath'd with new Scenes, Sir *William*'s great Care of having it
perfect and exactly perform'd, it produc'd to himself and Company
vast Profit.

These being all the Principal, which we call'd Stock-Plays; that
were Acted from the Time they Open'd the Theatre in 1662,[163] to
the beginning of *May*, 1665,[164] at which time the *Plague* began to
Rage: The Company ceas'd Acting; till the *Christmass* after the Fire

[159] Seen by Pepys on 3 April 1665.

[160] Character name accidentally omitted in the 1708 edition of *Roscius Anglicanus*; supplied here from the 1668 edition of the play.

[161] Downes appears to have confused this Roxolana with the character in *The Siege of Rhodes*. Hester Davenport had almost certainly left the stage by this time, and Mary Betterton created the role in *Mustapha*. Pepys reports her in the cast on 3 April.

[162] Otherwise unknown, unless she is the Jane Wiseman who wrote *Antiochus the Great* (1701).

[163] *Recte* June 1661.

[164] The theatres were closed by order of the Lord Chamberlain on 5 June 1665 (P.R.O. LC 5/138, p. 417).

in 1666.[165] Yet there were several other Plays Acted, from 1662, to 1665, both Old and Modern:[166] As a Comedy call'd, *A Trick to catch the Old One: The Sparagus Garden: Wit in a Constable. Tu Quoque: The Tragedy of King Lear*, as Mr. *Shakespear* Wrote it; before it was alter'd by Mr. *Tate*.[167] *The Slighted Maid: The Step-Mother*, both Written by Sir *Robert Stapleton: Law against Lovers*, by Sir *William Davenant*. *'Tis better than it was: Worse and Worse:* These Two Comedies were made out of *Spanish*, by the Earl of *Bristol*. *The Ghosts*, Wrote by Mr. *Holden: Pandora*, Wrote by Sir *William Killigrew*. The Company ending as I said with *Mustapha*, in *May* 1665, after a Year and Half's Discontinuance; they by Command began with the same Play again at Court: The *Christmass* after the Fire in 1666: And from thence continu'd again to Act at their Theatre in *Lincoln's-Inn-Fields*.

[27]

The first new Play that was Acted in 1666, was: *The Tragedy of Cambyses, King of Persia*, Wrote by Mr. *Settle*:[168] *Cambyses*, was

---

[165] After the plague the Duke's Company performed at Court as early as 18 October 1666. According to a newsletter (P.R.O. SP 29/179, no. 136), the theatres were permitted to reopen on 29 November. In all probability, both did so immediately, though our first definite record of a performance by the King's Company is on 7 December and by the Duke's Company not until 26 December.

[166] On the following list of plays, see Endnote 4.

[167] Shakespeare's tragedy was granted to the Duke's Company on 12 December 1660 (P.R.O. LC 5/137, pp. 343-344). In its original form it was seen by William Hammond ca. late January 1664 and by Nell Gwyn on 29 June 1675. Nahum Tate's happy-ending adaptation, which held the stage into the nineteenth century, probably received its première ca. October-December 1680.

[168] Downes is badly in error here: *Cambyses* almost undoubtedly received its première in 1670-71. The evidence is a 10 January 1671 performance in the Lord Chamberlain's lists; licensing and title page dates; a summer performance in Oxford; and Settle's comments in his preface to *Ibrahim* (pub. 1677). From publication, we would estimate a première in

perform'd by Mr. *Betterton*: *Prexaspes* the General, by Mr. *Harris*:
Prince *Smerdis*, Mr. *Young*: *Mandana*, by Mrs. *Betterton*: All the
other Parts, being perfectly well Acted, Succeeded six Days with a
full Audience.

After this the Company Reviv'd Three Comedies of *Mr. Sher-
ly*'s, viz.[169]

> *The Grateful Servant.*
> *The Witty Fair One.*
> *The School of Complements.*
> *The Woman's a Weather Cock.*

These Plays being perfectly well Perform'd; especially *Dulcino*
the Grateful Servant, being Acted by Mrs. *Long*; and the first time
she appear'd in Man's Habit, prov'd as Beneficial to the Company,
as several succeeding new Plays.[170]

---

early autumn 1670. Our best guess is that Downes associated this play
with a reopening after an enforced closing because it came soon after the
period of mourning for Charles II's sister, the Duchess of Orleans, who died
20 June 1670. This would help explain Downes' error, but it must be
regarded as conjecture. Downes does *not*, as *The London Stage* asserts (p.
179), claim that *Cambyses* was the first new play "acted at Dorset Garden
in 1666," a statement we are at a loss to explain.

[169] *The Grateful Servant* (1629) was seen by Dr. Edward Browne, probably in the spring of 1662. Jane Long would have been available to take
the breeches role at that time. Pepys saw the play 20 February 1669,
commenting, "which I have forgot that ever I did see." *The School of Com-
pliment* (1625) was performed at Court on 9 May 1667. No performance
date is known for *The Witty Fair One* (1628), though a prompt copy for a
Duke's Company production is preserved in the Bodleian. It has been
reproduced in facsimile by Edward A. Langhans in *Restoration Promptbooks* (Carbondale: Southern Illinois Univ. Press, 1981), chapter 15.
Downes is our only evidence of a revival of Nathan Field's *A Woman is a
Weather Cock* (ca. 1609) in this period.

[170] This paragraph was printed to the right of the preceding playlist in
the edition of 1708.

Richard the Third, or the English Princess, Wrote by Mr. *Carrol*,[171] was Excellently well Acted in every Part; chiefly, King *Richard*, by Mr. *Betterton*; Duke of *Richmond*, by Mr. *Harris*; Sir *William Stanly*, by Mr. *Smith*, Gain'd them an Additional Estimation, and the Applause from the Town, as well as profit to the whole Company.

King Henry the 5th, Wrote by the Earl of *Orrery*.[172] Mr. *Harris*, Acted the King: Mr. *Betterton*, *Owen Tudor*: Mr. *Smith*, Duke of *Burgundy*: Duke of *Bedford*, Mr. *Lilliston*: Earl of *Warwick*, Mr. *Angel*: *Clermont*, Mr. *Medburn*: Queen, Mrs. *Betterton*. This Play was Splendidly Cloath'd: The King, in the Duke of

[28]

York's Coronation Suit: *Owen Tudor*, in King *Charles*'s: Duke of *Burgundy*, in the Lord of *Oxford*'s, and the rest all New. It was Excellently Perform'd, and Acted 10 Days Successively.

---

[171] Pepys saw John Caryll's *The English Princess, or The Death of Richard the Third* on 7 March 1667, the only definite performance date. Downes is our only source for the cast.

[172] Pepys saw this play 13 August 1664 during its initial run. It was given a fancy revival when the theatres reopened in December 1666; Pepys comments on the elaborate costumes at that time (28 December). There are several differences between Downes' cast and that in the first edition of 1668. Medbourne's character was called the Count of Blamount. Downes may have thought of Mary Betterton as Queen because Katherine becomes Queen of England; she begins the play as a Princess. Downes gives Lilleston as Bedford, but by 1668 he was listed (as "Lylinston") for the smaller role of Bishop of Canterbury, and Underhill was Bedford. This discrepancy may be an error, or it may represent a cast change between 1664 and 1668. The edition of 1668 adds: Duke of Exeter—Cogan; Dauphin—Young; Earl of Chareloys—Cadiman; Constable of France—James Noke; De Chastel—Norris; Bishop of Arras—Samford; Colemore—Floyd; Queen of France—Mrs. Long; Princess Anne—Mrs. Davis; Countess of La Marr—Mrs. Norris. Bodleian MS Rawl. Poet 2 gives "Duke of Exeter—Mr. Nokes"; Robert Nokes probably preceded Cogan in the role.

After this my Lord *Orrery*, Writ Two Comedies: The first call'd *Gusman*;[173] the other *Mr. Anthony*.[174] *Gusman*, took very well, the other but indifferent. There being an odd sort of Duel in it, between Mr. *Nokes* and Mr. *Angel*, both Comicks meeting in the Field to fight, one came Arm'd with a *Blunderbus*, the other with a *Bow* and *Arrows*.[175]

Sir Martin Marral,[176] The Duke of *New-Castle*, giving Mr. *Dryden* a bare Translation of it, out of a Comedy of the Famous *French* Poet *Monseur Moleire*:[177] He Adapted the Part purposely for the Mouth of Mr. *Nokes*, and curiously Polishing the whole; Mr. *Smith*, Acting Sir *John Swallow*; Mr. *Young*, Lord *Dartmouth*; Mr. *Underhill*, Old *Moody*; Mr. *Harris*, *Warner*; Mrs. *Norris*, Lady *Dupe*; Mrs. *Millisent*, Madam *Davies*. All the Parts being very Just and Exactly perform'd, 'specially Sir *Martin* and his Man, Mr. *Smith*, and several others since have come very near him, but none Equall'd, nor yet Mr. *Nokes* in Sir *Martin*:[178] This Comedy was Crown'd with an

---

[173] Performed by 15 April 1669.

[174] Performed by 14 December 1669. A note by the fifth Earl of Orrery written some fifty years later and reprinted in *The London Stage* (Part 1, p. 168) says that the play lasted "only one Night." But since the fifth Earl asserts that it appeared after Orrery's death (when in fact he lived another ten years), the accuracy of this report is not beyond question.

[175] The duel in Act III involves Nokes as Mr. Anthony, armed with a long bow and arrows, and Angel as Cudden, armed with a pair of cudgels. Downes' "blunderbuss" is a flight of fancy—or, less probably, a record of a major production departure from Orrery's text.

[176] Pepys calls it "a play made by my Lord Duke of Newcastle, but as everybody says corrected by Dryden" (16 August 1667). On the authorship of this play, see F. H. Moore, "The Composition of *Sir Martin Mar-All*," *Essays in English Literature of the Classical Period presented to Dougald MacMillan*, ed. Daniel W. Patterson and Albrecht B. Strauss, *Studies in Philology*, Extra Series, 4 (January 1967), 27-38.

[177] Molière's *L'Étourdi* is an important source, but the first half of the play is in fact based on Philippe Quinault's *L'Amant indiscret*.

[178] Downes is our only source for the original cast. We do not know subsequent casts until very much later; on 24 June 1708 Bullock played Sir Martin, and Booth took Warner. Downes implies that William Smith

Excellent Entry: In the last Act at the Mask, by Mr. *Priest*[179] and Madam *Davies*; This, and *Love in a Tub*, got the Company more Money than any preceding Comedy.

She Wou'd if She Cou'd, Wrote by Sir *George Etheridge*;[180] *Courtall*, Acted by Mr. *Smith*: *Freeman*, Mr. *Young*: Sir *Joslin*, Mr. *Harris*: Sir

[29]

Oliver, Mr. *Nokes*: *Ariana*, Mrs. *Jenning*: *Gatty*, Mrs. *Davies*: Lady *Cockwood*, Mrs. *Shadwell*. It took well, but Inferior to *Love in a Tub*.

After this were Acted, *The Queen of Arragon*, and *Cupid's Revenge*.[181]

---

replaced Henry Harris as the clever servant Warner.

[179] On Josias Priest, who succeeded Luke Channel as dancing master for the Duke's and United Companies, see Selma Jeanne Cohen, "Theory and Practice of Theatrical Dancing in England in the Restoration and Early Eighteenth Century," *Bulletin of the New York Public Library*, 63 (1959), 541-554.

[180] The first recorded performance was 6 February 1668. Downes is our only source for the cast. Shadwell comments in his preface to *The Humorists* (pub. 1671) that "imperfect Action, had like to have destroy'd *She would if she could*, which I think . . . is the best Comedy that has been written since the Restauration of the Stage: And even that, for the imperfect representation of it at first, received such prejudice, that, had it not been for the favour of the *Court*, in all probability it had never got up again."

[181] William Habington's *The Queen of Aragon* (1640) was included in a list of old plays assigned to the Duke's Company on 20 August 1668 (LC 5/139, p. 375). It was mounted at Court on the Duke of York's birthday, 14 October 1668, with a special prologue and epilogue by Samuel Butler. Beaumont and Fletcher's *Cupid's Revenge* (ca. 1607-1612) was seen by Pepys on 17 August 1668 ("under the new name of *Love Despised*") three days before it was officially granted to the Duke's Company.

The Impertinents, or Sullen Lovers, Wrote by Mr. *Shadwell*;[182]
This Comedy being Admirably Acted: Especially, Sir *Positive At-all*,
by Mr. *Harris*: Poet *Ninny*, by Mr. *Nokes*: *Woodcock*, by Mr. *Angel*:
Standford and *Emilia*; the Sullen Lovers: One by Mr. *Smith*, and
the other by Mrs. *Shadwell*. This Play had wonderful Success,
being Acted 12 Days together.[183] When our Company were Com-
manded to *Dover*, in *May* 1670.[184] The King with all his Court,
meeting his Sister, the Dutchess of *Orleans* there. This Comedy
and *Sir Solomon Single*, pleas'd Madam the Dutchess, and the whole
Court extremely. The *French* Court wearing then Excessive short
Lac'd Coats; some Scarlet, some Blew, with Broad wast Belts; Mr.
Nokes having at that time one shorter than the *French* Fashion, to
Act Sir *Arthur Addle* in; the Duke of *Monmouth* gave Mr. *Nokes* his
Sword and Belt from his Side, and Buckled it on himself, on purpose
to Ape the *French*: That Mr. *Nokes* lookt more like a Drest up Ape,
than a Sir *Arthur*: Which upon his first Entrance on the Stage, put
the King and Court to an Excessive Laughter; at which the *French*
look'd very Shaggrin, to see themselves Ap'd by such a Buffoon as
Sir *Arthur*: Mr. *Nokes* kept the Dukes Sword to his Dying Day.

Sir Soloman Single, Wrote by Mr. *Carrol*,[185] Sir *Solomon* Acted
by Mr. *Betterton*: *Peregrine Woodland*,

---

[182] *The Sullen Lovers* premièred 2 May 1668 (Pepys). Downes is our
only source for the cast.

[183] We take this to mean a twelve-day run at the time of the première
in 1668 and have amended accordingly (see the Textual Notes), although
the *London Stage* calendar proves that the play could not have run twelve
consecutive days at the time of its première. Downes' contorted syntax
and the punctuation of the 1708 edition imply twelve days' performance at
Dover.

[184] This trip is confirmed by a newsletter (British Library Add. MS
36,916, fol. 182): "the Court . . . continues at dover till wensday. . . . The
Dukes players [who] have beene there all the time past came up [to Lon-
don] yesterday and the kings goe downe this day." On 17 August the Sec-
retary of the Treasury noted that the Duke's Company was to receive £500
for the trip (P.R.O. T29/625/131).

[185] John Caryll's *Sir Salomon* was probably first acted ca. April 1670.

[30]

by Mr. *Harris*: *Single*, by Mr. *Smith*: Mr. *Wary*, by Mr. *Sandford*: *Timothy*, by Mr. *Underhill*: *Betty*, by Mrs. *Johnson*: *Julia*, Mrs. *Betterton*. The Play being Singularly well Acted, it took 12 Days together.

The Woman made a Justice: Wrote by Mr. *Betterton*:[186] Mrs. *Long*, Acting the Justice so Charmingly; and the Comedy being perfect and justly Acted, so well pleas'd the Audience, it continu'd Acting 14 Days together: The Prologue being spoke to it each Day.

The Amorous Widow, or the Wanton Wife, Wrote by the same Author.[187] Mr. *Betterton*, Acted *Lovemore*: Mr. *Smith*, *Cuningham*: Mr. *Nokes*, *Barnaby Brittle*: The Widow, Mrs. *Betterton*: Mrs. *Long*, Mrs. *Brittle*: She Perform'd it so well, that none Equall'd her but Mrs. *Bracegirdle*.[188]

---

[186] The title of this lost play is confirmed by the Lord Chamberlain's lists at Harvard; the attribution is known only from Downes. The play was definitely performed by 19 February 1670; the date of première is unknown. Montague Summers, in "The Comedies of Thomas Betterton," *Notes and Queries*, 170 (1936), 454-456, offers the plausible speculation that the play was a translation-adaptation of Montfleury's *La femme juge et partie* (1669).

[187] Date of première unknown (ca. 1669?); definitely performed by late November 1670. Downes is our only source for the original cast. The play is a translation-adaptation whose main plot is based upon Thomas Corneille's *Le Baron d'Albikrac* (1667) and its subplot upon Molière's *George Dandin*. See John Harrington Smith, "Thomas Corneille to Betterton to Congreve," *Journal of English and Germanic Philology*, 45 (1946), 209-213.

[188] Summers (pp. 198-199) summarizes and denounces the story from the *Authentick Memoirs of . . . Mrs. Ann Oldfield*, 3rd ed. (London, 1730), pp. 19-22, about successive performances of *The Amorous Widow* in which Oldfield eclipsed Bracegirdle and forced her into premature retirement. The authors of the *Biographical Dictionary* (II, 275) wrongly ascribe this anecdote to the "William Egerton" (i.e., Curll) *Faithful Memoirs of . . . Mrs. Anne Oldfield* (1731), but nonetheless call it "probably true." No such occasion is documentable from the *London Stage* calendar, but Bracegirdle did retire suddenly in the middle of the 1706-07 season, and Oldfield took over

The Unjust Judge, or Appius and Virginia, done by the same Author.[189] *Virginius* Acted by Mr. *Betterton*, *Appius*, the Unjust Judge, by Mr. *Harris*: *Virginia*, by Mrs. *Betterton*. And all the other Parts *Exactly* perform'd, it lasted Successively 8 Days, and very frequently Acted afterwards.

The Man's the Master, Wrote by Sir *William Davenant*,[190] being the last Play he ever Wrote, he Dying presently after; and was Bury'd in *Westminster-Abby*, near Mr. *Chaucer*'s Monument, Our whole Company attending his Funeral.[191] This Comedy in general was very well Perform'd, especially, the *Master*, by Mr. *Harris*; the *Man*, by Mr. *Underhill*: Mr. *Harris* and Mr. *Sandford*, Singing the Epilogue like two Street Ballad-Singers.

[31]

Note, Mr. *Cademan* in this Play, not long after our Company began in *Dorset-Garden*; his Part being to Fight with Mr. *Harris*, was Unfortunately, with a sharp Foil pierc'd near the Eye, which so

---

Mrs. Brittle.

[189] Alternate title for *The Roman Virgin*, the first performance of which was 12 May 1669. The cast is known only from Downes. This play is an adaptation of Webster's *Appius and Virginia* (ca. 1608-1634?). Langbaine (p. 509) confirms Downes' attribution of the revisions to Betterton—"alter'd (as I have heard by Mr. *Carthwright*) by Mr. *Betterton*"—though Pepys, who saw the première, calls it "an old play" and the changes were probably minimal. For discussion, see Judith Milhous, "Thomas Betterton's Playwriting," *Bulletin of the New York Public Library*, 77 (1974), 375-392, esp. 383-384.

[190] Pepys saw what was probably the première on 26 March 1668. The play is a translation-adaptation of Scarron's *Jodelet, ou le maître valet*. Downes is the only source for the cast.

[191] Davenant died 7 April 1668; Pepys comments on his funeral procession on 9 April. Pepys implies that the Duke's Company did not perform that day, a mark of respect seldom accorded anyone in the theatre. Both theatres were dark the day of Dryden's funeral, though Rich was chided for renting out Dorset Garden for popular entertainments. See *The Patentee* (1700), Arnott and Robinson, no. 1315.

Maim'd both his Hand and his Speech, that he can make little use of either; for which Mischance, he has receiv'd a Pension ever since *1673,* being *35* Years a goe.[192]

This being the last New Play that was Acted in *Lincolns-Inn Fields,*[193] yet there were sundry others done there, from 1662, till the time they left that House:[194] As *Love's Kingdom,* Wrote by Mr. *Fleckno: The Royal Shepherdess,* by Mr. *Shadwell: Two Fools well met,* by Mr. *Lodwick Carlile:*[195] *The Coffee-house,* by Mr. *Sincerf:*

---

[192] Cademan's injury probably occurred on 9 August 1673. For discussion, see *The London Stage,* Part 1, p. 207. On 13 November 1684 Dame Mary Davenant testified that Cademan was allowed a pension of 30 shillings a week on account of his injury (P.R.O. C/6/250/28; her testimony is printed by Hotson, pp. 356-363). In "The Case of Philip Cademan" (ca. 1696), P.R.O. LC 7/3, fols. 26-27, the disabled actor states that after his injury "his Salary was continu'd until Mr. Rich had ye management of ye playhouse (as indeed all persons had it for their Lives that were disabled from Acting by Sickness or other Misfortunes)." Rich demanded that he "sit and deliver out Tickets which he did until he was disabled by Sickness in ye year 1695. But after he was restord to his health he offerd to serve in ye same Capacity . . . But Mr. Rich . . . has ever since denyd to pay him his Salary." Downes' account implies that the Lord Chamberlain ruled in Cademan's favor.

[193] A flagrant blunder: the move to Dorset Garden did not occur for more than three years, and many new plays were performed at Lincoln's Inn Fields in that time. Perhaps Downes means that the last performance at Lincoln's Inn Fields was of *The Man's the Master.*

[194] *Love's Kingdom* was licensed for publication 22 April 1664 and was probably performed earlier in the 1663-64 season. *The Royal Shepherdess* received its première 25 February 1669. *The Coffee-House* is the subtitle of Sir Thomas St. Serfe's *Tarugo's Wiles* (5 October 1667). "Mr. Stroude's" *All Plot* is lost and not otherwise known; it could have been staged at Lincoln's Inn Fields any time from 1661 to November 1671.

[195] Something is wrong here, this being the subtitle for James Carlile's *The Fortune Hunters* (1689). Unless Downes has misdated that play by twenty years and got the wrong Carlile to boot, we suspect that he means Lodowick Carlell's *The Fool Would be a Favourite* (ca. 1632-1638? pub. 1657), of which no Restoration revival is otherwise recorded.

All-Plot, or the Disguises, by Mr. *Stroude*: All which Expir'd the third Day, save the *Royal Shepherdess*, which liv'd Six.

Note, About the Year 1670, Mrs. *Aldridge*, after Mrs. *Lee*, after Lady *Slingsby*, also Mrs. *Leigh* Wife of Mr. *Antony Leigh*, Mr. *Crosby*, Mrs. *Johnson*, were entertain'd in the Dukes House.[196]

The new Theatre in *Dorset-Garden* being Finish'd, and our Company after Sir *William's* Death, being under the Rule and Dominion of his Widow the Lady *Davenant*, Mr. *Betterton*, and Mr. *Harris*, (Mr. *Charles Davenant* her Son Acting for her)[197] they remov'd from *Lincolns-Inn-Fields* thither. And on the Ninth Day of *November* 1671,[198] they open'd their new Theatre with *Sir Martin Marral*, which continu'd Acting 3 Days together, with a full Audience each Day; notwithstanding it had been Acted 30 Days before in *Lincolns-Inn-Fields*, and above 4 times at Court.[199]

---

[196] Apart from Downes' note, Mary Aldridge (who became Mrs. John Lee and subsequently Lady Slingsby) is first known from Aphra Behn's *The Forc'd Marriage* (September 1670). She apparently retired about 1685. Elinor, the wife of Anthony Leigh, may have been the actress Elinor Dixon before her marriage. She is first listed in *The Women's Conquest* (ca. September 1670), and acted until about 1707. Anthony Leigh (*d.* 1692) seems to have tried acting about 1671-72, but he did not establish himself solidly in the company until 1676. (John Lee's career overlapped Anthony Leigh's between ca. 1673 and 1677, but John Lee never became an important actor. He died sometime in 1680.) The first record of John Crosby is as Banacar, "a black Moor boy" in *Ignoramus* in November 1662; our next record of him is not until *The Forc'd Marriage* in September 1670. He left the stage about 1679. For Mrs. Johnson, see p. 70, below.

[197] Charles Davenant (1656-1714) was still a minor when his father died. He did not take an active part in the management of the Duke's Company until 1677, and he sold his entire interest to his brother Alexander in August 1687. Betterton and Harris, later Betterton and Smith, actually ran the business for Charles and his mother, Dame Mary.

[198] Both date and play are confirmed by an entry in a Lord Chamberlain's list. Since the next entry on that list is 13 November, Downes is probably right about the three-day run.

[199] According to the bills presented to the Lord Chamberlain's office for payment, the King saw *Sir Martin Mar-all* nine times before he attended it

[32]

Next was Acted *Love in a Tub*,[200] it was perform'd 2 Days together to a full Audience.

The first new Play Acted there, was *King Charles the VIII. of France*;[201] it was all new Cloath'd, yet lasted but 6 Days together, but 'twas Acted now and then afterwards.

The next new Comedy, was the *Mamamouchi, or the Citizen turn'd Gentleman*, Wrote by Mr. *Ravenscraft*:[202] *Trickmore*, and Fencing-Master, by Mr. *Harris*; *French* Tutor and Singing Master, by Mr. *Haines*: (He having Affronted Mr. *Hart*, he gave him a Discharge and then came into our House);[203] Old *Jorden*, Mr. *Nokes*;

---

at the opening of Dorset Garden. Only two of these performances, however, are definitely recorded as being at court, 3 February 1668 and 16 November 1668.

[200] I.e., Etherege's *The Comical Revenge* (1664). Payment for a performance of this play on 13 November 1671 on a Lord Chamberlain's list corroborates Downes.

[201] Crowne's play premièred in November 1671.

[202] The first recorded performance is 4 July 1672, but from publication norms a première in the period January-April seems likely. See "Dating Play Premières," p. 386. Q1672 adds: Young Jorden—Cademan; Cleverwit—Crosby; Marina—Mrs. Burroughs. It confirms Downes in all other roles save the French tutor, for whom it gives Maistre Jaques—Angel. With the exception of Jo Haines, everyone named would definitely have been available in 1672. Edward Angel died ca. 1673; when Haines took the role is hard to guess (see the next note). Harris played only one part; Trickmore first appears disguised as a fencing master. Haines could not have played both the music master and Jaques as the parts were written, since the two are on stage together in Act I.

[203] The date of this episode is impossible to pin down; it could fall anywhere between 1668 and 1673. Haines was apparently with the King's Company in December 1671 and appeared in *The Assignation* (May-November? 1672); his next definite appearance with them was not until May 1674. Haines was evidently with the Duke's Company for *Mr. Anthony* on 14 December 1669; exactly when he served another brief stint with them

Dr. *Cural*, Mr. *Sandford*; Sir *Symon Softhead*, Mr. *Underhill*; *Lucia*, Mrs. *Betterton*; *Betty Trickmore*, Mrs. *Leigh*: This Comedy was looked upon by the Criticks for a Foolish Play; yet it continu'd Acting 9 Days with a full House; upon the Sixth the House being very full: The Poet added 2 more Lines to his Epilogue, *viz.*

> *The Criticks come to Hiss, and Dam this Play,*
> *Yet spite of themselves they can't keep away.*

However Mr. *Nokes* in performing the *Mamomouchi* pleas'd the King and Court, next Sir *Martin*, above all Plays.

The third new Play Acted there was the *Gentleman Dancing-Master*, Wrote by Mr. *Witcherly*,[204] it lasted but 6 Days, being like't but indifferently, it was laid by to make Room for other new ones.

Note, Several of the Old Stock Plays were Acted between each of these 3 new Ones.

[33]

Epsom Wells, a Comedy Wrote by Mr. *Shadwell*:[205] Mr. *Rains*, was Acted by Mr. *Harris*: *Bevil*, by Mr. *Betterton*: *Woodly*, by Mr. *Smith*: Justice *Clod-pate*, Mr. *Underhill*: *Carolina*, Mrs. *Johnson*: *Lucia*, Mrs. *Gibbs*: Mrs. *Jilt*, by Mrs. *Betterton*: Mr. *Nokes*, Mr. *Bisket*: Mr. *Angel*, *Fribble*. This Play in general being Admirably Acted, produc'd great Profit to the Company.

Note, Mrs. *Johnson* in this Comedy, Dancing a Jigg so Charming well, Loves power in a little time after Coerc'd her to Dance more Charming, else-where.[206]

----

cannot be determined with any confidence. Autumn 1672 is a possibility; the season of 1673-74 (after Angel's death) is another. See *Biographical Dictionary*, VII, 7-10.

[204] The first recorded performance is 6 February 1672.

[205] The first recorded performance is 2 December 1672. Downes is our only source for the cast, though Underhill is confirmed by Cibber's praise for him as Clodpate (*Apology*, I, 155).

[206] Mrs. Johnson's first known role is Betty in *Sir Salomon* (ca. April 1670). According to the *Biographical Dictionary*, "elsewhere was in the

A Comedy call'd *The Reformation*, Written by a Master of Arts in *Cambridge*;[207] The Reformation in the Play, being the Reverse to the Laws of Morality and Virtue; it quickly made its Exit, to make way for a Moral one.

The Tragedy of Macbeth, alter'd by Sir *William Davenant*;[208] being drest in all it's Finery, as new Cloath's, new Scenes, Machines, as flyings for the Witches; with all the Singing and Dancing in it: The first Compos'd by Mr. *Lock*, the other by Mr. *Channell* and Mr. *Joseph Preist*;[209] it being all Excellently perform'd, being in the nature of an Opera, it Recompenc'd double the

---

arms of, among others, the Earl of Peterborough" (VIII, 169-170). She had evidently left the stage by the end of 1673.

[207] *The Reformation* is a satire on Dryden, in particular on his *Marriage A-la-Mode*. It was published in 1673; from topicality and publication norms we would guess at a première in late spring or summer 1672. The author was Joseph Arrowsmith, who received his M.A. in 1670 and became Master of St. John's Hospital and Rector of St. John's, Bedford (*Alumni Cantabrigienses*, comp. John Venn and J. A. Venn, Part 1, 4 vols. [Cambridge: Cambridge Univ. Press, 1922-1927], I, 42). The play is by no means bawdy, and Downes' censure of the reformation imposed is quite unjustified. He may have been thinking of the scene in which Leandro swears on a copy of Ovid "to reform *Venice* according to the Pattern of *England*," so help him Cupid (p. 17).

[208] Pepys saw what was probably Davenant's adaptation on 5 November 1664. A major revival, perhaps augmented with additional music, occurred in December 1666. See Roger Fiske, "The 'Macbeth' Music," *Music and Letters*, 45 (1964), 114-125. A performance on 18 February 1673 seems to be the first record of the Dorset Garden production of the opera, which was spectacular enough to provoke a King's Company parody in the epilogue to Duffett's *The Empress of Morocco* later that year.

[209] On Matthew Locke (1621?-1677), see the article by Murray Lefkowitz in *The New Grove* (XI, 107-117), who concludes that Locke wrote some of the music for *Macbeth*, but by no means all of it. Luke Channel (*fl.* 1653-1691?) was the Duke's Company's first recorded dancing master, sworn on 23 November 1664 (P.R.O. LC 3/25, p. 162) but probably with them earlier. Downes' report on *Macbeth* is Channel's last known theatrical activity. On Josias (not Joseph) Priest, see p. 63, above.

Expence; it proves still a lasting Play.

Note, That this Tragedy, *King Lear* and the *Tempest*, were Acted in *Lincolns-Inn-Fields*; *Lear*, being Acted exactly as Mr. *Shakespear* Wrote it; as likewise the *Tempest* alter'd by Sir *William Davenant* and Mr. *Dryden*, before 'twas made into an Opera.[210]

Loves Jealousy, and	Written by Mr. *Nevil*
The Morning Ramble.[211]	*Pain.*

[34]

Both were very well Acted, but after their first run, were laid aside, to make Room for others; the Company having then plenty of new Poets.

The Jealous Bridegroom, Wrote by Mrs. *Bhen*,[212] a good Play and lasted six Days; but this made its Exit too, to give Room for a greater, *The Tempest*.

Note, In this Play, Mr. *Otway* the Poet having an Inclination to turn Actor; Mrs. *Bhen* gave him the King in the Play, for a Probation Part, but he being not us'd to the Stage; the full House put him to such a Sweat and Tremendous, Agony, being dash't, spoilt him for an Actor.[213] Mr. *Nat. Lee*, had the same Fate in Acting *Duncan*,

---

[210] The Dryden-Davenant *Tempest* received its première 7 November 1667 (Pepys) and proved a tremendous success.

[211] Henry Nevil Payne's *The Fatal Jealousie* appears on an LC list under the date 3 August 1672; *The Morning Ramble* is entered for a performance 4 November 1672. Neither première is known.

[212] Aphra Behn's *The Forc'd Marriage; or, The Jealous Bridegroom* is first recorded in an LC list under the date 20 September 1670. There is no confirmatory evidence that it was followed by a revival of *The Tempest* in 1670.

[213] According to Q1671 the King was played by Westwood. J. C. Ghosh doubts that Otway needed to work before his father died in February 1671, and he suggests that if Downes identified the play correctly Otway might have taken the part in an unrecorded revival (ca. spring 1674?). See *The*

in *Macbeth*, ruin'd him for an Actor too.[214] I must not forget my self, being Listed for an Actor in Sir *William Davenant*'s Company in *Lincolns-Inn-Fields*: The very first Day of opening the House there, with the *Siege of Rhodes*, being to Act *Haly*; (The King, Duke of *York*, and all the Nobility in the House, and the first time the King was in a Publick Theatre);[215] The sight of that *August* presence, spoil'd me for an Actor too. But being so in the Company of two such Eminent Poets, as they prov'd afterward, made my Disgrace so much the less; from that time, their Genius set them upon Poetry: The first Wrote *Alcibiades*; The later, the *Tragedy of Nero*; the one for the Duke's, the other for the King's House.

The Year after in 1673.[216] *The Tempest, or the Inchanted Island*, made into an Opera by Mr. *Shadwell*,[217] having all New in

---

Works of Thomas Otway, 2 vols. (Oxford: Clarendon Press, 1932), I, 12n.

[214] Lee is listed as Duncan in the 1673 and 1674 editions and in the Yale MS. He is also given as Captain of the Watch in the Dramatis Personae in Q1673 of Henry Nevil Payne's *The Fatal Jealousie*, known to have been performed in August 1672.

[215] On Downes' abortive career as an actor, see W. J. Lawrence, *Old Theatre Days and Ways* (London: Harrap, 1935), pp. 144-145. Because Pepys mentions a eunuch "so much out that he was hissed off the stage" on 2 July 1661, Lawrence doubts that Downes' attack of stage fright occurred at the première in the presence of the King. But Downes may well have remained in the cast for a few days.

[216] Downes means 1673/4. *The London Stage*, Part 1, p. 215, assigns the première to 30 April 1674, but the evidence is tenuous, and performance any time after mid-March seems possible. Dryden alludes sneeringly to *The Tempest* in his prologue for the opening of Drury Lane, 26 March, though whether it had been performed or was just being puffed in advance of its première we cannot be certain.

[217] This statement has occasioned long and acrimonious dispute. For a convenient reprint of the two texts (1670 and 1674) and a sensible summary, see *After the Tempest*, intro. by George Robert Guffey (Los Angeles: William Andrews Clark Memorial Library, 1969). The actual changes in the text necessary to convert the Dryden-Davenant play into an "opera" were quite minimal, amounting to some cuts, a bit of dramatic cobblework, and the addition of a new song. We see no reason to doubt Downes'

it; as Scenes, Machines; particularly, one Scene Painted with *Myri-ads* of *Ariel* Spirits; and another flying away, with a Table Furnisht out with Fruits, Sweet meats, and all sorts of Viands;

[35]

just when Duke *Trinculo* and his Companions, were going to Dinner; all things perform'd in it so Admirably well, that not any succeeding Opera got more Money.[218]

About this time the Company was very much Recruited,[219] having lost by Death Mr. *Joseph Price*, Mr. *Lovell*, Mr. *Lilliston*, Mr. *Robert Nokes*, Mr. *Mosely*, Mr. *Coggan*, Mr. *Floid*, Mr. *Gib-bons*; Mrs. *Davenport*, Mrs. *Davies*, Mrs. *Jennings*, &c. The three last by force of Love were Erept the Stage: In their Rooms came in Mr. *Anthony Lee*,[220] Mr. *Gillo*, Mr. *Jevon*, Mr. *Percival*, Mr. *Wil-liams*, who came in a Boy, and serv'd Mr. *Harris*,[221] Mr. *Boman* a Boy likewise: Mrs. *Barry*, Mrs. *Currer*, Mrs. *Butler*, Mrs. *Slaughter*,

---

assertion that Shadwell was responsible for this bit of revamping. Shad-well did not, however, substantially rewrite the adaptation of 1667 (pub-lished in 1670). We are grateful to Mr. Andrew James Pinnock for gener-ously sharing with us the results of his investigation of the textual history of the play.

[218] On the staggering financial investment by the Duke's Company in mounting its major semi-opera productions, see Judith Milhous, "The Mul-timedia Spectacular on the Restoration Stage," *British Theatre and the Other Arts, 1660-1800*, ed. Shirley Strum Kenny (Washington, D.C.: Folger Books, 1984), pp. 41-66. *The Tempest* seems to have been relatively inex-pensive (though fancily staged), which helped make it more profitable than such shows as *Psyche* and *The Fairy-Queen*. To judge from fragmentary performance records, *The Tempest* was the most popular work on the Lon-don stage prior to *The Beggar's Opera* in 1728.

[219] On Downes' lists of people who left the company and those who replaced them, see Endnotes 5 and 6.

[220] I.e., the great comedian Anthony Leigh.

[221] This statement is evidence that the company was still using, at least in part, the traditional apprenticeship system of recruitment and training.

Mrs. *Knapper*, Mrs. *Twiford*.

After the *Tempest*, came the *Siege of Constantinople*, Wrote by Mr. *Nevill Pain.*[222]

Then the *Conquest of China by the Tartars*; by Mr. *Settle;*[223] in this Play Mr. *Jevon* Acting a *Chinese* Prince and Commander in it, and being in the Battle, Vanquisht by the *Tartars*; he was by his Part to fall upon the point of his Sword and Kill himself, rather than be a Prisoner by the *Tartars*: Mr. *Jevon* instead of falling on the point of his Sword, laid it in the Scabbard at length upon the Ground and fell upon't, saying, now I am Dead; which put the Author into such a Fret, it made him speak Treble, instead of Double. *Jevons* answer was; did not you bid me fall upon my Sword.

In *February* 1673. The long expected Opera of *Psyche*,[224] came forth in all her Ornaments; new Scenes, new Machines, new Cloaths, new *French* Dances: This Opera was Splendidly set out, especially in Scenes; the Charge of which

[36]

amounted to above 800*l*. It had a Continuance of Performance about 8 Days together, it prov'd very Beneficial to the Company; yet the *Tempest* got them more Money.

---

[222] This play was seen by both Charles II and Nell Gwyn on 2 November 1674.

[223] Acted by 28 May 1675. Q1676 gives Theinmingus—Gillow; Zungteus—Harris; Palexus—Norris; King of China—Medbourn; Quitazo—Smith; Lycungus—Sandford; Orunda—Mrs. Betterton; Alcinda—Mrs. Corer [Currer]; Amavanga—Mary Lee; Vangona—Mrs. Spencer. Downes' anecdote implies that Jevon acted "*Legozun*, a Prince of *China*." The episode described is part of a group suicide in Act V in which the defeated Chinese King and Princes "all fall on their Swords" (p. 61).

[224] Shadwell's adaptation of the Lully-Molière comedy-ballet received its première on 27 February 1674/5. Downes probably meant February 1673/4, a year too early. His error is magnified by Summers, who printed "1672," a mistake quoted by the editors of *The London Stage*.

After this *Sir Patient Fancy*[225] was Acted.

Then the *Rover*.[226] Both Wrote by Mrs. *Bhen*.

Alcibiades,[227] the first Play that Mr. *Otway* Wrote.

Madam Fickle,[228] by Mr. *Durfey*.

Then *Don Carlos Prince of Spain*;[229] the Second Play Wrote by Mr. *Otway*: The King, was perform'd by Mr. *Betterton*: Prince, by Mr. *Smith*: *Don John* of *Austria*, by Mr. *Harris*: *Gomez*, Mr. *Medburn*: Queen, Madam *Slingsby*; and all the Parts being admirably Acted, it lasted successively 10 Days; it got more Money than any preceding Modern Tragedy.[230]

After this in 1676. *The Man of Mode, or Sir Fopling Flutter*[231]

---

[225] Acted by 17 January 1678.

[226] Acted by 24 March 1677.

[227] Probably first acted in mid-October 1675.

[228] Seen by Nell Gwyn on 4 November 1676.

[229] Acted by 8 June 1676. Q1676 confirms Downes' cast, giving Mrs. Mary Lee for the Queen (she did not become Lady Slingsby until 1680) and adds: Marquis of Posa—Crosby; Duchess of Eboli—Mrs. Shadwell; Henrietta—Mrs. Gibbs; Garcia—Mrs. Gillow; Officer—Norris. Mrs. Gillow may have been Mary, wife of Thomas Gillow. She is listed for a few minor roles between 1675 and 1678.

[230] On 19 June 1732 Barton Booth wrote to Aaron Hill concerning "the Taste of the Town": "Mr. *Betterton* observ'd to me many Years ago, that *Don Carlos* succeeded much better than either *Venice Preserv'd* or the *Orphan*, and was infinitely more applauded and follow'd for many Years." *A Collection of Letters . . . written . . . To the Late Aaron Hill, Esq*; (London: W. Owen, 1751), p. 82.

[231] Acted in March 1676. Q1676 gives no actors' names. Following Wilson, the editors of *The London Stage* doubt that Mrs. Barry took Loveit this early, hypothesizing that the role originally belonged to Mary Lee. This is possible, but by no means necessarily true. Barry performed in *Alcibiades* in autumn 1675, and several parts are documented for her in the summer and autumn of 1676. Loveit was a more important role than we might expect for an inexperienced actress, but Barry could well have been thrust into it by the temporary unavailability of another performer. See Robert D. Hume, "Elizabeth Barry's First Roles and the Cast of *The Man of Mode*," *Theatre History Studies*, 5 (1985), 16-19.

was Acted: *Dorimant*, by Mr. *Betterton*: *Medly*, Mr. *Harris*: Sir *Fopling*, by Mr. *Smith*: Old *Bellair*, Mr. *Leigh*: Young *Bellair*, Mr. *Jevon*: Mrs. *Lovit*, Mrs. *Barry*: *Bellinda*, Mrs. *Betterton*: Lady *Woodvil*, Mrs. *Leigh*: *Emilia*, Mrs. *Twiford*: This Comedy being well Cloath'd and well Acted, got a great deal of Money.

The Soldiers Fortune,[232] Wrote by Mr. *Otway*.

Then the *Fond Husband*,[233] by Mr. *Durfey*.

These two Comedies took extraordinary well, and being perfectly Acted; got the Company great Reputation and Profit.

Circe,[234] an Opera Wrote by Dr. *Davenant*; *Orestes*, was Acted by Mr. *Betterton*: *Pylades*, Mr. *Williams*: *Ithacus*, Mr. *Smith*: *Thoas*, Mr. *Harris*: *Circe*, Lady *Slingsby*: *Iphigenia*, Mrs. *Betterton*: *Osmida*, Mrs. *Twiford*. All the Musick was set by Mr. *Banister*, and being well Perform'd, it

[37]

answer'd the Expectation of the Company.

The Siege of Troy.[235]	By Mr. *Banks*.
Anna Bullen.[236]	

---

[232] Acted by mid-June 1680.

[233] Acted by 31 May 1677. *The London Stage*, Part 1, p. 257, records a report in *The Guardian* (15 June 1713) that Charles II attended three of the first five nights of this play. Extant bills show that he attended only 31 May and 8 June. He was, however, sufficiently enthusiastic that he set Dryden to writing another like it—*The Kind Keeper, or Mr. Limberham* (March 1678). See *The Letters of John Dryden*, ed. Charles E. Ward (Durham: Duke Univ. Press, 1942), no. 5.

[234] Acted by 12 May 1677. Q1677 gives no actors' names. At the time of the première, Lady Slingsby was still Mrs. Mary Lee.

[235] John Banks' *The Destruction of Troy*, premièred by November 1678.

[236] Banks' *Vertue Betray'd*, acted by late March 1682.

The feign'd Curtezans.[237]	Both by Mrs. *Bhen.*
The City Heiress.[238]	

These Four were well Acted; Three of them liv'd but a short time: but *Ann Bullen* prov'd a Stock-Play.

Timon of Athens,[239] alter'd by Mr. *Shadwell*; 'twas very well Acted, and the Musick in't well Perform'd; it wonderfully pleas'd the Court and City; being an Excellent Moral.

The Libertine, and *Virtuoso*:[240] Both Wrote by Mr. *Shadwell*; they were both very well Acted, and got the Company great Reputation. The *Libertine* perform'd by Mr. *Betterton* Crown'd the Play.

The Spanish Fryar,[241] Wrote by Mr. *Dryden*; 'twas Admirably Acted, and produc'd vast Profit to the Company.

Oedipus King of Thebes,[242] Wrote by Mr. *Nat. Lee*, and Mr. *Dryden*: The last Writing the first two *Acts*, and the first the 3 last.

---

[237] Probably acted ca. March 1679 (but possibly as early as May 1677).

[238] Acted by late April or early May 1682.

[239] Acted ca. January 1678. At least part of the music for the original production was written by Louis Grabu. Purcell reset the Act II masque of Cupid and Bacchus, probably for a revival by the Patent Company ca. June 1695. For discussion of the complex history of the music for this play, see Curtis Alexander Price, *Henry Purcell and the London Stage* (Cambridge: Cambridge Univ. Press, 1984), pp. 89-96.

[240] The former was seen by Nell Gwyn on 12 June 1675 and probably received its première about a month earlier (see Judith Milhous, "The Duke's Company's Profits, 1675-1677," *Theatre Notebook*, 22 [1978], 76-88); the latter was definitely acted by 25 May 1676.

[241] Acted by 1 November 1680.

[242] Acted ca. September-October 1678. Dryden states in *The Vindication . . . of . . . The Duke of Guise* (London: Tonson, 1683), p. 42: "I writ the first and third Acts of *Oedipus*, and drew the *Scenary* of the *whole Play*." The edition of 1679 gives the rest of the cast: Adrastus—Smith; Creon— Samford; Tiresias—Harris; Haemon—Crosby; Alcander—Williams; Diocles—Norris; Pyracmon—Boman; Phorbas—Gillo; Ghost of Lajus—Williams; Eurydice—Mrs. Lee; Manto—Mrs. Evans.

This Play was Admirably well Acted; especially the Parts of *Oedipus* and *Jocasta*: One by Mr. *Betterton*, the other by Mrs. *Betterton*; it took prodigiously, being Acted 10 Days together.

The Orphan, or the Unhappy Marriage;[243] Wrote by Mr. *Otway*: *Castalio* Acted by Mr. *Betterton*: *Polidor*, Mr. *Williams*: *Chamont*, Mr. *Smith*: *Chaplain*, Mr. *Percival*: *Monimia*, Mrs. *Barry*: *Serina*, Mrs. *Monfort*. All the Parts being Admirably done, especially the Part of *Monimia*: This,

[38]

and *Belvidera* in *Venice preserv'd, or a Plot Discover'd*;[244] together with *Isabella*, in the *Fatal Marriage*:[245] These three Parts, gain'd her the Name of Famous Mrs. *Barry*, both at Court and City; for when ever She Acted any of those three Parts, she forc'd Tears from the Eyes of her Auditory, especially those who have any Sense of Pity for the Distress't.

These 3 Plays, by their Excellent performances, took above all the Modern Plays that succeeded.

Titus and Berenice,[246] Wrote by the same Author, consisting of 3 *Acts*: With the *Farce* of the *Cheats of Scapin* at the end: This Play, with the *Farce*, being perfectly well Acted; had good Success.

---

[243] Acted ca. late February 1680. Q1680 gives Serina—Mrs. Boteler (i.e., Charlotte Butler) and adds: Acasto—Gillow; Ernesto—Norris; Paulino—Wiltshire; Cordelio—"By the little Girl" (possibly Anne Bracegirdle); Florella—Mrs. Osborn. Downes' cast probably reflects performances ca. 1684 or later, when Susanna Percival (who married Mountfort in 1686) evidently took the role of Serina over from Charlotte Butler, who was off the stage for some time in the mid-1680s.

[244] Acted by 9 February 1682.

[245] Acted ca. February 1694.

[246] Probably acted in early November 1676. Translated from Racine. Because Otway did not add the customary underplot, the play was too short to stand by itself, and as Downes notes he added a translation of Molière's *Les Fourberies de Scapin*, thus accidentally anticipating the mainpiece/afterpiece pattern that was to become the norm in the eighteenth century.

Theodosius, or the Force of Love,[247] Wrote by Mr. *Nathaniel Lee*: *Varanes,* the *Persian* Prince, Acted by Mr. *Betterton: Marcian* the General, Mr. *Smith: Theodosius,* Mr. *Williams: Athenais,* Mrs. *Barry*: All the Parts in't being perfectly perform'd, with several Entertainments of Singing; Compos'd by the Famous Master Mr. *Henry Purcell,* (being the first he e'er Compos'd for the Stage)[248] made it a living and Gainful Play to the Company: The Court; especially the Ladies, by their daily charming presence, gave it great Encouragement.

Note, Mr. *Lee,* Wrote the *Tragedy of Nero.*[249] *The Court of Augustus,*[250] for *Drury-Lane* House. *The Prince of Cleve*[251] for *Dorset-Garden,* being well Acted, but succeeded not so well as the others.[252]

The *Lancashire Witches,*[253] Acted in 1681, made by Mr. *Shadwell,* being a kind of Opera,[254] having several *Machines* of Flyings for the Witches, and other Diverting Contrivances in't: All being well perform'd, it prov'd beyond

---

[247] Acted ca. late spring 1680. Q1680 adds: Lucius—Wiltshire; Atticus—Bowman; Leontine—Leitherfull; Pulcheria—Mrs. Betterton. This is Leitherfull's only known role.

[248] For discussion, see Price, *Henry Purcell and the London Stage,* pp. 30-37.

[249] Acted at Drury Lane by 16 May 1674, when the King attended.

[250] I.e., *Gloriana, or the Court of Augustus Caesar,* performed before the King at Drury Lane on 29 January 1676.

[251] Lee's *The Princess of Cleve* was probably performed ca. December 1682, though not published until 1689. See Robert D. Hume, "The Satiric Design of Nat. Lee's *The Princess of Cleve,*" *Journal of English and Germanic Philology,* 75 (1976), 117-138.

[252] This paragraph was printed in small type to the left of the previous one in the edition of 1708.

[253] Performed ca. March-June 1681, it achieved considerable success despite harsh cuts by the censor (see Shadwell's note "To the Reader" in Q1682).

[254] "Opera" in the sense of fancy display piece, a multi-media spectacular.

[39]

Expectation; very Beneficial to the Poet and *Actors*.

All the preceding Plays, being the chief that were Acted in *Dorset-Garden*, from *November* 1671, to the Year 1682; at which time the Patentees of each Company United Patents;[255] and by so Incorporating the Duke's Company were made the King's Company, and immediately remov'd to the Theatre Royal in *Drury-Lane*.[256]

Upon this Union, Mr. *Hart* being the Heart of the Company under Mr. *Killigrew*'s Patent never Acted more, by reason of his Malady; being Afflicted with the Stone and Gravel, of which he Dy'd some time after:[257] Having a Sallary of 40 Shillings a Week to the Day of his Death.[258] But the Remnant of that Company; as,

---

[255] The "Articles of Union" of 4 May 1682 by which the patents were united are printed by Fitzgerald, I, 154-158 (his unstated source is British Library Add. MS 20,726, fols. 10-13v). The agreement specifies that Charles Killigrew will dissolve the King's Company within six days; will deliver the stock of playbooks and other possessions (scenery excepted) to Charles Davenant; and will yield tenancy of the Drury Lane theatre. In return, Charles Davenant engages to pay £3 for the use of Drury Lane every time *either* theatre is used and to grant Charles Killigrew 3/20 of the profits of the joint acting company. For a complete transcription of the documents connected with the Killigrew family's share in the patent, the King's Company, and the United Company, see Judith Milhous and Robert D. Hume, "Charles Killigrew's 'Abstract of Title to the Playhouse': British Library Add. MS 20,726, Fols. 1-14," *Theatre History Studies*, 6 (1986), 57-71.

[256] See note 99, above.

[257] Hart died 18 August 1683 (Luttrell).

[258] Genest (I, 375) assumes that Downes' figure is wrong and that the actual salary was 30 shillings per week. The basis for this objection is the agreement signed 14 October 1681 between Hart and Kynaston on one side and the Duke's Company managers on the other, printed by Gildon, pp. 8-9. Hart and Kynaston were promised 5 shillings per acting day (i.e., 30 shillings for a full six-day week) in return for their signing over their rights in the King's Company's stock of scenery, costumes, and plays, and agreeing not to perform for the King's Company. We do not know, how-

Major *Mohun*, Mr. *Cartwright*, Mr. *Kynaston*, Mr. *Griffin*, Mr. *Goodman*, Mr. *Duke Watson*, Mr. *Powel* Senior, Mr. *Wiltshire*, Mrs. *Corey*, Mrs. *Bowtell*, Mrs. *Cook*, Mrs. *Monfort*,[259] &c.[260]

Note, now Mr. *Monfort* and Mr. *Carlile*, were grown to the Maturity of good *Actors*.[261]

The mixt Company then Reviv'd the several old and Modern Plays,[262] that were the Propriety of Mr. *Killigrew*, as, *Rule a Wife*,

---

ever, exactly what arrangements were made a year later at the time of the union, and Downes' figure of 40 shillings may well be correct. Either must be regarded as a generous retirement allowance.

[259] I.e., Susanna Percival (who was to marry William Mountfort in 1686).

[260] Something is missing from Downes' text here—evidently a statement to the effect that these actors joined the United Company. Mohun was offered only "20s. a day when they have occasion to use him." He successfully petitioned the King for an order granting him "the same Conditions as Mr Hart and Mr Kinaston" (P.R.O. LC 5/191, fols. 102v-103). Cartwright acted only occasionally (*Biographical Dictionary*, III, 91), as did Goodman (John Harold Wilson, *Mr. Goodman the Player* [Pittsburgh: Univ. of Pittsburgh Press, 1964], pp. 82-85). We have no definite record of Watson acting again in London until 1697-98 (if it is the same Watson); W. S. Clark shows that he had moved to Dublin by 1684-85. (See *The Early Irish Stage* [Oxford: Clarendon Press, 1955], pp. 88-89.) Elizabeth Bowtell apparently did not act with the United Company until 1688. Thus Downes lists the principal remaining performers of the King's Company, but though the United Company may technically have agreed to accept all of them, several did not get full-time work with the new company.

[261] William Mountfort's first known role was the "Boy" in *The Counterfeits* (1678), where he is called "Young Mumford"; he performed Jack the Barber's boy in *The Revenge* (1680). His first adult role was Corso in *The Duke of Guise* (November 1682). James Carlile's first known role was Aumale in *The Duke of Guise*.

[262] We have records of United Company performances during the 1680s of all of these plays save *Bartholomew Fair* (dates specified in Endnote 7). This is excellent confirmation of Downes' list, though in all probability most of the revivals occurred in the first two or three years after the union. Access to the plays which had been the property of the King's Company

and have a Wife:[263] Mr. *Betterton* Acting *Michael Perez*: *Don Leon*, Mr. *Smith*: *Cacofogo*, Mr. *Cartwright*: *Margaretta*, Mrs. *Barry*: *Estiphania*, Mrs. *Cook*: Next,[264]

> *The Scornful Lady.*
> *The Plain Dealer.*
> *The Mock Astrologer.*
> *The Jovial Crew.*
> *The Beggars Bush.*

[40]

> *Bartholomew-Fair.*
> *The Moor of Venice.*
> *Rollo.*
> *The Humorous Lieutenant.*
> *The Double Marriage.* With divers others.

Next new Play was the Tragedy of *Valentinian*,[265] wrote by the

---

was plainly a great incentive to the Duke's Company to offer reasonable terms for a union, and the small number of new plays mounted for several years after 1682 suggests heavy reliance on revivals of King's Company plays. Among the "divers others" known to have been produced by the United Company between 1682 and 1686 are *The Chances*, *The Northern Lass*, *The Mistaken Beauty*, *The Destruction of Jerusalem*, *The Silent Woman*, *A King and no King*, *The Rival Queens*, *The Committee*, *All for Love*, and *The Rehearsal*.

[263] Performed by the Duke's Company 1 November 1682 at the Inner Temple even before the union formally took effect.

[264] On the following revivals, see Endnote 7.

[265] Performed at Court 11 February 1684. It was by no means the first "new Play" after the union: Downes ignores *The Duke of Guise* (November 1682), *City Politiques* (January 1683), *Dame Dobson* (May 1683), *The Atheist* (ca. May? 1683), and *Constantine the Great* (November 1683). *Valentinian* was written much earlier, and a cast in the extant MSS implies performance or intended performance by the King's Company ca. 1675-76 (British Library Add. MS 28,692, and Folger MS V.b. 233).

Lord *Rochester*, from *Beaumont* and *Fletcher*. Mr. *Goodman* Acted *Valentinian*: Mr. *Betterton*, *Æcius*: Mr. *Kynaston*, *Maximus*: Mr. *Griffin*, *Pontius*: Madam *Barry*, *Lucina*, &c. The well performance, and the vast Interest the Author made in Town,[266] Crown'd the Play, with great Gain of Reputation; and Profit to the *Actors*.

In *Anno* 1685. The Opera of *Albion and Albanius*[267] was perform'd; wrote by Mr. *Dryden*, and Compos'd by Monsieur *Grabue*: This being perform'd on a very Unlucky Day, being the Day the *Duke* of *Monmouth*, Landed in the *West*: The Nation being in a great Consternation, it was perform'd but Six times, which not Answering half the Charge they were at, Involv'd the Company very much in Debt.[268]

The first new Comedy after King *James* came to the *Crown*, was *Sir Courtly Nice*,[269] wrote by Mr. *Crown*: Sir *Courtly*, Acted by Mr. *Mounfort*: Hothead, Mr. *Underhill*: Testimony, Mr. *Gillo*: Lord *Beaugard*,[270] Mr. *Kynaston*: Surly, by Mr. *Griffin*: Sir *Nicholas Callico*, by the Famous Mr. *Antony Leigh*: Leonora, Madam *Barry*, &c. This Comedy being

[41]

---

[266] The Earl of Rochester died on 26 July 1680. Davies therefore objects to this statement, and Knight criticizes Waldron for printing it (1886, pp. xxviii-xxix). But Downes probably meant only that the identity of the author created great public interest.

[267] Performed by 3 June 1685. Grabu's full score was elegantly published in 1687.

[268] A letter cited in *The London Stage*, Part 1, p. 334, reports that the company invested £4000 in staging the work, and that they proposed to charge "a guyny a place" in the boxes, "and the Pitt at halfe." The effect of the truncation of the run of this opera by Monmouth's ill-fated invasion is evident in the financial records that have been preserved. See Judith Milhous, "United Company Finances, 1682-1692," *Theatre Research International*, 7 (1981-82), 37-53. The company did not risk another opera until *The Prophetess* in 1690.

[269] Acted by 9 May 1685. Downes is our only source for the original cast.

[270] *Recte* Lord Bellguard (Q1685).

justly Acted, and the Characters in't new, Crown'd it with a general Applause: Sir *Courtly* was so nicely Perform'd, that not any succeeding, but Mr. *Cyber*[271] has Equall'd him.

Note, Mr. *Griffin*[272] so Excell'd in *Surly,* Sir *Edward Belfond,* The *Plain Dealer,* none succeeding in the 2 former have Equall'd him, except his Predecessor Mr. *Hart* in the latter.[273]

The Squire of Alsatia,[274] a Comedy Wrote by Mr. *Shadwell:* Sir *William Belfond,* done by Mr. *Leigh:* Sir *Edward,* Mr. *Griffin:* The Squire by Mr. *Nokes,* afterwards by Mr. *Jevon:*[275] *Belfond* Junior, Mr. *Mounfort:* Mrs. *Termigant,* Mrs. *Boutel: Lucia,* Mrs.

---

[271] When Colley Cibber inherited the role (following Mountfort's death in December 1692) is uncertain, but he was definitely performing it by 30 October 1703.

[272] Downes evidently means that no one equalled Griffin in Surly and Sir Edward Belfond and that only his predecessor Hart equalled him as Manly.

[273] This paragraph was printed in small type to the left of the preceding one (i.e., on page 40 in the edition of 1708).

[274] Contradictory evidence points to May 2, 4, or 5 as the date of the première. See *The London Stage,* Part 1, pp. 363-364. The epilogue says that the poet "begs that you will often grace his Play, / And lets you know *Munday*'s his visiting day." We take his visiting day to be the author's benefit, which suggests that the première was intended to be Friday, 4 May. (Dates in *The London Stage* for May 1688 are a day off: 4 May was a Friday, not a Thursday.)

[275] Q1688 gives Jevon, which implies that Jevon (who died later in the year) replaced Nokes very early indeed after the first run, if not during it. The quarto was advertised in the *Term Catalogue* for Easter 1688. See Edward Arber, ed., *The Term Catalogues, 1668-1709,* 3 vols. (London: privately printed, 1903-1906), II, 223-224. Logically, of course, "The Squire by Mr. Jevon, afterwards by Mr. Nokes" would make better sense. Possibly Downes accidentally reversed the sequence. Otherwise Q1688 confirms Downes' cast and adds: Truman—Bowman; Cheatly—Samford; Shamwell—Powell Jun.; Captain Hackum—Bright; Scrapeall—Freeman; Attorney—Powell Sr.; Lolpoop—Underhill; Termagant—Alexander [i.e., John Verbruggen?]; Teresia—Mrs. Knight; Isabella—Mrs. Mountford. Later editions add Ruth—Mrs. Corey.

Bracegirdle. This Play by its Excellent Acting, being often Honour'd with the presence of Chancellour *Jefferies*,[276] and other great Persons; had an Uninterrupted run of 13 Days together.

Note, Mr. *Leigh* was Eminent in this part of Sir *William*, & *Scapin*. Old *Fumble*. Sir *Jolly Jumble*. *Mercury* in *Amphitrion*. Sir *Formal*, *Spanish* Fryar, *Pandarus* in *Troilus and Cressida*.[277]

Note, The Poet receiv'd for his third Day in the House in *Drury-Lane* at single Prizes 130*l.* which was the greatest Receipt they ever had at that House at single Prizes.[278]

About this time, there were several other new Plays Acted. As,

The True Widow.[279] | All but *Amphitrion*;

---

[276] George Jeffreys, first Baron Jeffreys of Wem (1648-1689), best known as principal judge in the "bloody assizes" that followed the suppression of Monmouth's invasion in 1685.

[277] This paragraph was printed in small type to the right of the preceding one in the edition of 1708. The roles mentioned are as follows: Scapin in Otway's *The Cheats of Scapin* (November 1676); Old Fumble in Durfey's *A Fond Husband* (May 1677); Sir Jolly Jumble in Otway's *The Souldiers Fortune* (June 1680); Mercury in Dryden's *Amphitryon* (October 1690); Sir Formal Trifle in Shadwell's *The Virtuoso* (May 1676); Dominic in Dryden's *The Spanish Fryar* (November 1680); Pandarus in Dryden's *Troilus and Cressida* (ca. late winter 1679?).

[278] Whether Downes means that total receipts at single (rather than "raised") prices were £130 or that Shadwell's net after the deduction of "house charges" (about £30 at this period) was £130, we cannot be certain. The seating capacity of the Drury Lane theatre in this period remains a subject of dispute.

[279] Not a new play. Shadwell's *A True Widow* failed in March (?) 1678, and Downes had evidently forgotten about it. His statement implies an otherwise unrecorded revival by the United Company ca. 1688-89, which is likely enough after the triumph of *The Squire of Alsatia* in May 1688. A new edition in the spring of 1689 tends to confirm such a revival.

Sir Anthony Love.[280]

The Scowrers.[281]

Amphytrion.[283]

Love in, and Love

    out of Fashion.[284]

Greenwich Park.[285]

Cleomenes.[286]

Troilus and Cressida.[287]

Cæsar Borgia.[288]

which succeeding but

indifferently,[282] I Omit

the Persons Names that

Acted in these Plays;

this proving a Stock-Play.

---

[280] By Thomas Southerne; acted ca. November 1690.

[281] By Shadwell; ca. December 1690.

[282] Downes' memory is certainly at fault concerning Southerne's *Sir Anthony Love*, a roaring success in 1690, though how well it held the stage is questionable. *Troilus and Cressida* remained a stock play, *Amphitryon* was revived regularly for more than three-quarters of a century, and *Greenwich-Park* was regularly revived into the eighteenth century.

[283] Dryden's comedy was acted by 21 October 1690.

[284] Probably Bulteel's *Amorous Orontus*. See "Lost English Plays," no. 69. First acted by the King's Company ca. 1664-65. Downes implies a revival in the season of 1690-91 or thereabouts.

[285] Mountfort's comedy was acted ca. April 1691.

[286] Dryden's tragedy was acted in mid-April 1692.

[287] Dryden's adaptation was first performed by the Duke's Company ca. late winter 1679. Downes had evidently forgotten about it; he implies a revival in the season of 1690-91 or thereabouts.

[288] Lee's play was not new, having originally been performed by the Duke's Company ca. spring 1679. Downes implies a revival about 1690-91.

[42]

The Old Bachelor,[289] wrote	All 3 good Plays;
by Mr. *Congreve.*	and by their just
The Fatal Marriage, or	Performances; specially,
Innocent Adultry;[290] by	Mr. *Doggets* and Madam
Mr. *Southern.*	*Barry*'s Unparrell'd.[291]
The Double Dealer;[292] by	
Mr. *Congreve.*	

The Boarding School;[293] Wrote by Mr. *Durfy*, it took well being justly Acted.

The Marriage Hater Match'd,[294] Wrote by the same Author:

---

[289] An "extraordinary" success when premièred in March 1693 (*Gentleman's Journal*), it remained a stock play for many decades.

[290] Southerne's play, an immediate and lasting success, received its première ca. February 1694.

[291] Doggett performed Fondlewife, Fernando, and Sir Paul Plyant; Barry took Laetitia, Isabella, and Lady Touchwood in these three plays. Doggett's Fondlewife and Barry's Isabella were among their most celebrated roles.

[292] Congreve's second comedy was acted ca. November 1693. Though it proved a *succès d'estime* (see *The Letters of John Dryden*, no. 28, 12 December 1693), it was a disappointment after the triumph of *The Old Batchelour.*

[293] Durfey's *Love for Money*, acted by March 1691. Its great popularity was later sneered at in the *Lacedemonian Mercury* for 11 March 1691/2.

[294] Durfey's comedy was acted ca. January 1692. Doggett's success as Solon was such that it became his nickname for a time. See Dryden's let-

There Mr. *Dogget* perform'd the part of *Solon* inimitably; likewise his Part in the *Boarding-School*.

King Arthur[295] an Opera, wrote by Mr. *Dryden*; it was Excellently Adorn'd with Scenes and Machines: The Musical Part set by Famous Mr. *Henry Purcel*; and Dances made by Mr. *Jo. Priest*: The Play and Musick pleas'd the Court and City, and being well perform'd, twas very Gainful to the Company.

The Prophetess, or Dioclesian[296] an Opera, wrote by Mr. *Betterton*; being set out with Coastly Scenes, Machines and Cloaths: The Vocal and Instrumental Musick, done by Mr. *Purcel*; and Dances by Mr. *Priest*; it gratify'd the Expectation of Court and City; and got the Author great Reputation.

The Fairy Queen,[297] made into an Opera, from a Comedy of Mr. *Shakespears*: This in Ornaments was Superior to the other Two; especially in Cloaths, for all the Singers and Dancers, Scenes, Machines and Decorations, all most profusely set off; and excellently perform'd, chiefly the Instrumental and Vocal part

[43]

Compos'd by the said Mr. *Purcel*, and Dances by Mr. *Priest*. The Court and Town were wonderfully satisfy'd with it; but the Expences in setting it out being so great, the Company got very little by it.

Note, Between these Opera's there were several other Plays Acted, both Old and Modern.[298] As,

---

ter of 9 May 1693 (*Letters*, no. 24).

[295] Premièred in early June 1691.

[296] Performed in June 1690.

[297] Premièred 2 May 1692. Luttrell states that "the clothes, scenes, and musick cost 3000*l*" (II, 435). The text (an alteration of *A Midsummer Night's Dream*) has often been attributed to Elkanah Settle, but there is no solid evidence for this ascription. See "Attribution Problems," no. 20.

[298] The following list is probably out of place. All of these plays *could* have been performed by the United Company between June 1690 and May 1692, but known performances suggest the likelihood of the list's belonging on page 41 of the original edition, before or after *The Squire of Alsatia*,

Bury Fair.[299]
Wit without Money.[300]
The Taming of a Shrew.[301]
The Maiden Queen.[302]
The Mistress, by Sir *Charles Sydly.*[303]
Island Princess.[304]
A Sea Voyage.[305]
The English Fryar, by Mr. *Crown.*[306]
Bussy D'Ambois.[307]
The Massacre of Paris, &c.[308]

---

which seems to fall in the midst of it. With the exception of *Bussy*, all of the plays on which we have performance evidence appear to fall in the years 1685-1690.

[299] Shadwell's comedy received its première ca. April 1689.

[300] This is our only evidence for a revival of Fletcher's play in the late eighties or early nineties.

[301] Presumably John Lacy's adaptation, *Sauny the Scot*, originally performed by the King's Company by April 1667 and revived at Drury Lane in 1697-98. Downes implies a United Company revival in the later 1680s.

[302] Dryden's *Secret-Love* (1667) is known to have been performed at Drury Lane on 14 December 1686, and at Court the next day. It may well have been a stock play at this period.

[303] Sedley's *Bellamira* evidently had a stormy reception during its first run in May 1687. We have no evidence of a revival.

[304] Probably Nahum Tate's revision of the 1668 adaptation of Fletcher's play, performed in April 1687. There is no evidence of a revival until Motteux's operatic version of February 1699 at Drury Lane.

[305] Probably Durfey's adaptation, *A Commonwealth of Women*, premièred in August 1685, though an otherwise unrecorded revival of Fletcher's original circa 1689-90 cannot be ruled out. We have no evidence of a revival of Durfey's play.

[306] Premièred in March 1690.

[307] Presumably Durfey's adaptation, staged ca. March 1691.

[308] Lee's play (written at the time of the Popish Plot and banned) received its first performance around the beginning of November 1689. An unsuccessful revival occurred at Drury Lane in August 1716.

Some time after, a difference happening between the United Patentees, and the chief *Actors*:[309] As Mr. *Betterton*; Mrs. *Barry* and Mrs. *Bracegirdle*; the latter complaining of Oppression from the former; they for Redress, Appeal'd to my Lord of *Dorset*,[310] then Lord Chamberlain, for Justice; who Espousing the Cause of the Actors, with the assistance of Sir *Robert Howard*,[311] finding their Complaints just, procur'd from King *William*, a Seperate License[312] for Mr. *Congreve*,[313] Mr. *Betterton*, Mrs. *Bracegirdle* and Mrs. *Barry*, and others, to set up a new Company, calling it the New Theatre in *Lincolns-Inn-Fields*;[314] and the House being fitted up

---

[309] "The Petition of the Players" (ca. November 1694) and "The Reply of the Patentees" (10 December 1694) are both printed in full from the manuscripts in P.R.O. LC 7/3, fols. 2-4, 8-20, by Milhous, *Thomas Betterton*, pp. 225-246.

[310] On Dorset, who served as Lord Chamberlain from 1689 to 1697, see Brice Harris, *Charles Sackville, Sixth Earl of Dorset: Patron and Poet of the Restoration* (Urbana: Univ. of Illinois Press, 1940). Dorset was a man with literary pretensions who, according to a letter by Nell Gwyn in June 1678, had spent a lot of time drinking beer in the playhouse with Thomas Shadwell and Henry Harris. For the full text, see John Harold Wilson, *Nell Gwyn: Royal Mistress* (New York: Pellegrini and Cudahy, 1952), pp. 287-288.

[311] Author of *The Committee* (1662) and other plays, one of the original King's Company shareholders, and Dryden's brother-in-law, Howard was asked to serve as mediator. On 7 December 1694 the Lord Chamberlain called a meeting at Howard's house in London for "Munday morninge next" (P.R.O. LC 5/151, p. 397).

[312] Issued on 25 March 1695 and preserved in MS copies in P.R.O. LC 7/1, p. 38 and 7/3, fol. 7; printed by Nicoll, I, 361.

[313] Downes is in error in saying that Congreve was among those named in the Lincoln's Inn Fields license; all of those included were actors. Congreve was, however, closely associated with the company, and he withdrew *Love for Love* from the patent company to give it to the rebels. See Cibber, *Apology*, I, 197.

[314] Information about the "second" Lincoln's Inn Fields remains maddeningly scanty. We have no specific figures on its dimensions or capacity.

from a Tennis-Court, they Open'd it the last Day of *April*, 1695, with a new Comedy: Call'd,

[44]

Love for Love,[315] Wrote by Mr. *Congreve*; this Comedy was Superior in Success, than most of the precedent Plays: *Valentine*, Acted by Mr. *Betterton*; *Scandall*, Mr. *Smith*; *Foresight*, Mr. *Sandford*; *Sampson*, Mr. *Underhill*; *Ben* the Saylor, Mr. *Dogget*; *Jeremy*, Mr. *Bowen*; Mrs. *Frail*, by Madam *Barry*; *Tattle*, Mr. *Boman*; *Angelica*, Mrs. *Bracegirdle*: This Comedy being Extraordinary well Acted, chiefly the Part of *Ben* the Sailor, it took 13 Days Successively.

The Principal new Plays[316] that succeeded this from *April* 1695, to the Year 1704. Were,

Lovers Luck,[317] a Comedy, Wrote by Captain *Dilke*, which fill'd the House 6 Days together, and above 50*l*. the 8*th*, the Day it was left off.
   The Grand Cyrus,[318] wrote by Mr. *Banks*; it was a good Play; but Mr. *Smith* having a long part in it, fell Sick upon the Fourth Day and Dy'd, upon that it lay by, and ne'er has bin Acted since.
   The Mourning Bride,[319] a Tragedy, wrote by Mr. *Congreve*; had such Success, that it continu'd Acting Uninterrupted 13 Days

---

From a variety of disparaging references, we may deduce that it was small: the prologue to *The Fatal Discovery* (1698) calls it "*Betterton*'s Booth," and the author of *A Comparison Between the Two Stages* alludes to "*Homer*'s Illiads in a Nut-shel" in describing an opera production there (p. 22).
   [315] Q1695 confirms Downes' cast and adds: Trapland—Triffusis; Buckram—Freeman; Mrs. Foresight—Mrs. Bowman; Miss Prue—Mrs. Ayliff; Nurse—Mrs. Leigh; Jenny—Mrs. Lawson.
   [316] Downes naturally lists only the plays mounted by his own company.
   [317] Ca. December 1695.
   [318] Premièred in mid-December 1695. Smith's part was Cyaxares.
   [319] Mid-February 1697.

together.

Boadicea, the Brittish Queen,[320] wrote by Mr. *Hopkins*; 'twas a well Writ Play in an *Ovidean* Stile in Verse; it was lik'd and got the Company Money.

Heroick Love,[321] Wrote by Mr. *George Greenvil,*[322] Superlatively Writ; a very good Tragedy, well Acted, and mightily pleas'd the Court and City.

Love's a Jest,[323] a Comedy, done by Mr. *Mateox*; succeeded well, being well Acted, and got the Company Reputation and Money.

The Anatomist, or Sham Doctor,[324] had prosperous

[45]

Success, and remains a living Play to this Day; 'twas done by Mr. *Ravenscroft.*

Don Quixot, both Parts made into one,[325] by Mr. *Durfey,* Mrs. *Bracegirdle* Acting, and her excellent Singing in't; the Play in general being well Perform'd, 'tis little Inferior to any of the preceding

---

[320] Published in 1697; date of first performance unknown. A letter from Elizabeth Barry to Lady Lisburne in the possession of William W. Appleton proves that it was performed on 25 October 1697. However, Curtis A. Price points out to us that the chronological organization of Yale Univ. Filmer MS 9 (which contains Forcer's act music for the play) strongly implies a première between Congreve's *Love for Love* in April 1695 and Dilke's *The City Lady* in December 1696.

[321] Acted ca. January 1698.

[322] I.e., George Granville, later Baron Lansdowne.

[323] Ca. June 1696. The author was Peter Anthony Motteux.

[324] November 1696.

[325] As originally staged by the United Company in May 1694, Durfey's *Don Quixote* comprised two separate five-act plays given on different days. Downes naturally ignores part 3, staged by the rival Drury Lane company ca. November 1695. Summers (pp. 255-256) expresses incredulity at the idea of a combination, but Downes is correct. On 5 July 1700 the Lincoln's Inn Fields company advertised *Don Quixote,* "both Parts being made into one by the Author."

Comedies.

The She-Gallants,[326] a Comedy, wrote by Mr. *George Greenvil*, when he was very Young: Extraordinary Witty, and well Acted; but offending the Ears of some Ladies who set up for Chastity, it made its Exit. And gave place to,

Iphigenia a Tragedy,[327] wrote by Mr. *Dennis*, a good Tragedy and well Acted; but answer'd not the Expences they were at in Cloathing it.

The Fate of Capua,[328] wrote by Mr. *Southern*, better to Read then Act; 'twas well Acted, but answer'd not the Companies Expectation.

Justice Busy,[329] a Comedy wrote by Mr. *Crown*; 'twas well Acted, yet prov'd not a living Play: However Mrs. *Bracegirdle*, by a Potent and Magnetick Charm in performing a Song in't; caus'd *the Stones of the Streets to fly in the Men's Faces.*[330]

The Way of the World,[331] a Comedy wrote by Mr. *Congreve*,

---

[326] Ca. January 1696. Granville asserts in his preface to Q1696 that he wrote the play "in *France* about twelve Years past"—i.e., ca. 1684 at the age of seventeen. Since his source, Campistron's *L'Amante Amant*, was acted in 1684, this is just possible. By the standards of 1696, *The She-Gallants* was relatively risqué.

[327] December 1699. The success of this play was damaged by its running head-to-head against Abel Boyer's *Achilles; or, Iphigenia in Aulis* at Drury Lane. On this collision of Iphigenias, see *A Comparison Between the Two Stages*, pp. 24-25.

[328] Staged in April 1700.

[329] Date uncertain (ca. 1699-1700); see "Lost English Plays," no. 88. On the seven preserved songs, see B. J. McMullin, "The Songs from John Crowne's *Justice Buisy, or The Gentleman-Quack*," *Review of English Studies*, n.s. 28 (1977), 168-175.

[330] This phrase is a distortion of a line from one of the songs in the play.

[331] Premièred in early March 1700. Congreve's play did not succeed as the company had hoped it would, but it was not a failure, and contrary to general belief it was revived within two years. See Robert D. Hume, "A Revival of *The Way of the World* in December 1701 or January 1702," *Theatre Notebook*, 26 (1971), 30-36.

twas curiously Acted; Madam *Bracegirdle* performing her Part so exactly and just, gain'd the Applause of Court and City; but being too Keen a Satyr, had not the Success the Company Expected.

The Ambitious Step-mother,[332] done by Mr. *Rowe*; 'twas very well Acted, especially the Parts of Mr. *Betterton*, Mr. *Booth* and Madam *Barry*; the Play answer'd the Companies expectation.

Tamerlane, wrote by the same Author,[333] in

[46]

general well Acted; but chiefly the Parts of Mr. *Betterton*, *Vanbruggen*, Mr. *Powel*, Madam *Bracegirdle* and *Barry*; which made it a Stock-Play.

The Fair Penitent,[334] by the same Author, a very good Play for three *Acts*; but failing in the two last, answer'd not their Expectation.

The Biter,[335] a Farce, wrote by the same Author, it had a six Days run; the six Days running it out of Breath, it Sicken'd and Expir'd.

Abra-mule, wrote by Mr. *Trap* of *Oxford*;[336] a very good Play and exceedingly well Acted.

These being all the chiefest new Plays,[337] that have been Acted by Mr. *Betterton*'s Company, since its Separation from Mr. *Rich* in

---

[332] Ca. December 1700. Q1701 gives: Memnon—Betterton; Artaban—Booth; Artemisa—Mrs. Barry.

[333] Ca. December 1701. Performed annually for many years on King William's birthday (4 November). Q1702 gives: Tamerlane—Betterton; Bajazet—Verbruggen; Moneses—Powell; Selima—Mrs. Bracegirdle; Arpasia—Mrs. Barry.

[334] Acted ca. May 1703. Downes' view notwithstanding, *The Fair Penitent* returned to the stage in 1715 and rapidly became one of the most popular stock tragedies, holding the boards throughout the eighteenth century.

[335] Ca. late November 1704.

[336] January 1704.

[337] Downes omits only a few plays that now seem important, principally Vanbrugh's *The Provok'd Wife* (ca. April 1697) and Dennis and Eccles' opera, *Rinaldo and Armida* (December 1698).

the Year 1695. The Names of several of the *Actors* I have not mention'd or offer'd to your View, as in the others, by Reason the late
Acting of them, makes them live in your Memories.

   Note, In the space of Ten Years past, Mr. *Betterton* to gratify
the desires and Fancies of the Nobility and Gentry; procur'd from
Abroad the best Dances and Singers,[338] as, Monsieur *L'Abbe*,[339]
Madam *Sublini*,[340] Monsieur *Balon*,[341] *Margarita Delpine*,[342] *Maria
Gallia*[343] and divers others; who being Exorbitantly Expensive,

---

[338] Both Cibber and Gildon comment sourly on the expense and dramatic irrelevancy of these entr'acte entertainers. See Cibber, *Apology*, I,
316-318, and Gildon, p. 155.

[339] L'Abbé first came to London in May 1698—something we know only
because he gave a performance before William III, and in reporting this
event the *Post-Boy* mentioned that he "is lately come over and Dances now
at the Play-house" (issue of 13-17 May). He subsequently served as principal dancer and dancing master at Lincoln's Inn Fields before quarrelling
with management in 1703. He then performed at both theatres before
returning to Paris in 1705.

[340] Marie-Thérèse Subligny (ca. 1666-ca. 1735), a principal performer
in the ballet at the Paris Opera, 1688-1707. Betterton brought her to London for about six weeks as an entr'acte performer in December 1701 and
January 1702. See Hume, "A Revival of *The Way of the World*" (note 331,
above).

[341] A principal performer at the Paris Opera, Balon was brought over
for five weeks in April and May 1699 at a cost of 400 guineas salary plus
a gift of 100 guineas from Lord Cholmley (Luttrell, 8 April). *A Comparison Between the Two Stages* says that "the Town ran mad" to see Balon,
adding that "the prizes were rais'd to an extravagant degree to bear the
extravagant rate they allow'd him" (p. 29).

[342] Margherita de l'Épine (*d.* 1746), one of the principal Italian singers
active in England before the opening of the Royal Academy in 1720. She
may have been the "Italian woman" who performed in London in 1693; see
D. F. Cook, "Françoise Marguérite de l'Epine: The Italian Lady?" *Theatre
Notebook*, 35 (1981), 58-73, 104-113. She performed regularly in London
from the spring of 1703 (*Biographical Dictionary*, IV, 292-296).

[343] Prominent Italian singer, active in London from June 1703; from ca.
1704 wife of the musician Giuseppe Fedeli Saggione (*Biographical Diction-*

produc'd small Profit to him and his Company, but vast Gain to themselves; Madam *Delpine* since her Arrival in *England*, by Modest Computation; having got by the Stage and Gentry, above 10000 Guineas.

Note, From *Candlemas* 1704, to the 23*d*, of *April* 1706. There were 4 Plays commanded to be Acted at Court at St. *James's*,[344] by the *Actors* of both Houses, *viz.*[345]

First, *All for Love*:[346] Mr. *Betterton*, Acting *Marc.*

[47]

Antony; Mr. *Vantbrugg*,[347] *Ventidius*; Mr. *Wilks*, *Dolabella*; Mr. *Booth*, *Alexas* the Eunuch; Mrs. *Barry*, *Cleopatra*; Mrs. *Bracegirdle*, *Octavia*: All the other Parts being exactly done, and the Court very well pleas'd.

The Second was, *Sir Solomon, or the Cautious Coxcomb*:[348] Mr.

---

ary, V, 439-440).

[344] A confusing statement, since the fourth of the command performances Downes names came on 5 February 1706.

[345] *All for Love* and *Sir Salomon* were definitely in the repertory of both companies. We have evidence of *Merry Wives* and *The Anatomist* only at Lincoln's Inn Fields in the years 1700-1706, but records are very sketchy until late 1705. Probably *Merry Wives* was in the repertory at both theatres, but the joint production of *The Anatomist* is surprising, since it was a Lincoln's Inn Fields play of 1696 and ought not to have been available to Drury Lane. Anne had evidently seen the play in November 1696; it was published with a "Prologue to Her Royal Highness by Mr Motteux." The mixed casts in these command performances are a clear sign of improved relations between the two companies. See Milhous, *Thomas Betterton*, Chapter 6.

[346] Performed Monday 7 February 1704. For Congreve's prologue on the occasion, see *The Complete Works of William Congreve*, ed. Montague Summers, 4 vols. (London: Nonesuch, 1923), IV, 72-73.

[347] I.e., John Verbruggen (not John Vanbrugh).

[348] Caryll's *Sir Salomon* was performed Monday 28 February 1704. Confirmed by a letter from Elizabeth Coke to Thomas Coke, who adds, "They say the Queen and Prince was both extremely diverted with it" (*The*

Betterton, Acting Sir *Solomon*; Mr. *Wilks*, *Peregrine*; Mr. *Booth*, Young *Single*; Mr. *Dogget*, Sir *Arthur Addle*; Mr. *Johnson*, Justice *Wary*; Mr. *Pinkethman*, *Ralph*; Mr. *Underhill*, *Timothy*; Mrs. *Brace-girdle*, *Julia*; Mrs. *Mounfort*, *Betty*: The whole being well perform'd, it gave great Satisfaction.

The next was, *The Merry Wives of Windsor*,[349] Acted the 23d, of *April*, the Queens Coronation Day: Mr. *Betterton*, Acting Sir *John Falstaff*; Sir *Hugh*, by Mr. *Dogget*; Mr. *Page*, by Mr. *Vanbruggen*; Mr. *Ford*, by Mr. *Powel*; Dr. *Caius*, Mr. *Pinkethman*; the Host, Mr. *Bullock*; Mrs. *Page*, Mrs. *Barry*; Mrs. *Ford*, Mrs. *Bracegirdle*; Mrs. *Ann Page*, Mrs. *Bradshaw*.

The last was, *The Anatomist, or Sham-Doctor*;[350] it was perform'd on *Shrove-Tuesday*, the Queen's Birth Day, it being done by the *Actors* of both Houses, and perfectly Perform'd; there being an Additional Entertainment[351] in't of the best Singers and Dancers, Foreign and *English*:[352] As *Margarita D'elpine*, *Maria Gallia*, Mrs. *Lindsey*, Mrs. *Hudson* and Mr. *Leveridge*, and others: The Dances were perform'd by Monsieur *L'Abbe*; Mr. *Ruel*; Monsieur *Cherrier*; Mrs. *Elford*; Miss *Campion*; Mrs. *Ruel* and *Devonshire* Girl: Twas very well lik'd by the whole Court.

About the end of 1704, Mr. *Betterton* Assign'd his License, and his whole Company over to

[48]

London Stage, Part 2, I, 59). By this date Susanna Mountfort had become Mrs. Verbruggen.

[349] Given 23 April 1705 (if Downes gives the command performances in order) or 23 April 1706 (if we go by his headnote on p. 97). Vanbrugh's company performed the play at the Haymarket theatre on 23 April 1705—possibly a warmup for a court performance later that evening. *The London Stage*, Part 2, I, 64-65, assigns this performance to 24 April 1704.

[350] Performed Tuesday 5 February 1706.

[351] As originally produced in 1696, *The Anatomist* was filled out with a masque, Motteux's *The Loves of Mars and Venus* (music by Eccles and Finger). Whether the same 'Entertainment' was used for the command performance we cannot be certain.

[352] On the following list of singers and dancers, see Endnote 8.

Captain *Vantbrugg* to Act under his,[353] at the Theatre in the *Hay Market.*[354]

And upon the 9*th*, of *April* 1705. Captain *Vantbrugg* open'd his new Theatre in the *Hay-Market*, with a Foreign Opera,[355] Perform'd by a new set of Singers,[356] Arriv'd from *Italy*; (the worst that e're came from thence) for it lasted but 5 Days, and they being lik'd but indifferently by the Gentry; they in a little time marcht back to their own Country.

The first Play Acted there, was *The Gamester.*[357] Then the

------

[353] We have no other evidence of the nature of the deal struck between the Lincoln's Inn Fields actors and Vanbrugh. In fact, a new license was issued to Vanbrugh and Congreve on 14 December 1704 (P.R.O. LC 5/154, p. 35). It has been printed in *Congreve: Letters and Documents*, no. 70.

[354] On the financing and construction of the new theatre, see Judith Milhous, "New Light on Vanbrugh's Haymarket Theatre Project," *Theatre Survey*, 17 (1976), 143-161. For the best reconstruction of the Haymarket theatre as it existed between 1705 and the alterations of 1709, see Graham F. Barlow, "From Tennis Court to Opera House," diss. Univ. of Glasgow, 1983, Vol. I, Part 3. See also Richard Leacroft, *The Development of the English Playhouse* (London: Eyre Methuen, 1973), pp. 99-105.

[355] Jakob Greber's *Gli Amori D'Ergasto*. The performance was evidently in Italian. On problems posed by this work and occasion, see Curtis A. Price, "The Critical Decade for English Music Drama, 1700-1710," *Harvard Library Bulletin*, 26 (1978), esp. pp. 46-47; and Milhous, *Thomas Betterton*, pp. 198-199.

[356] Identity unknown, and much disputed. Price ("The Critical Decade," p. 47) suggests that "Vanbrugh and Congreve may have imported one or two Italian singers during the frantic preparations for the opening of their theatre, but it is likely that they assembled most of their shabby cast from among the foreigners at the rival Drury Lane theatre."

[357] *The Gamester*, a reform comedy, had premièred with great success in February 1705 at Lincoln's Inn Fields. It was performed at the Haymarket on 27 April. Betterton's *The Amorous Widow* (ca. 1669?) had been performed at Lincoln's Inn Fields on 20 February 1705 and had become part of the Haymarket repertory by 12 November that year. Tate's *Duke and no Duke* (1684) was performed at Lincoln's Inn Fields on 12, 15, and 22 February 1704 and at the Haymarket on 16 November 1705. Ether-

Wanton Wife. Next, *Duke and no Duke*. After that, *She wou'd, if She Cou'd*; and half a Score of their old Plays,[358] Acted in old Cloaths, the Company brought from *Lincolns-Inn-Fields*. The Audiencies falling off extremly with entertaining the Gentry with such old Ware, whereas, had they Open'd the House at first, with a good new *English* Opera, or a new Play; they wou'd have preserv'd the Favour of Court and City, and gain'd Reputation and Profit to themselves.[359]

The first new Play Acted there, Was the *Conquest of Spain*;[360] the beginning of *May* 1705, Written by Mrs. *Pix*, it had not the life of a Stock-Play, for it Expir'd the 6*th*, Day.

The next new one was *Ulysses*,[361] wrote by Mr. *Row*: The Play

---

ege's *She wou'd* (1668) was performed regularly by the rival company at Drury Lane this spring (15 and 19 March and 5 July) and was definitely revived at the Haymarket by 7 December 1705.

[358] Because Vanbrugh had not yet started to advertise regularly in the *Daily Courant*, Downes' statement about revivals cannot be proved, but it is compatible with such performance records as we possess. The only definite performance known between 11 April (the third day of *Ergasto*) and 24 April is *The Indian Emperour* on the 14th. Lacking contrary evidence, we should probably accept Downes' assertion that *The Gamester, The Amorous Widow, A Duke and no Duke, She wou'd if she cou'd*, and several other "old Plays" filled the two-week interval. *The London Stage* does not even mention this passage.

[359] This need not be taken as mere chauvinism. The considerable success of Granville's *The British Enchanters* a year later proves that traditional English semi-opera still appealed to London audiences. On the late history of semi-opera, see Robert D. Hume, "Opera in London, 1695-1706," *British Theatre and the Other Arts*, ed. Kenny, pp. 67-91.

[360] Probably acted between 12 and 22 May 1705, after which known performances of other plays preclude the run Downes mentions. It was not "the first new play Acted there," an honor belonging to an anonymous farce called *The Consultation* (not printed—lost), which survived only two days, 24 and 25 April.

[361] Premièred 23 November 1705. We have record of seven performances in the initial run and three more in the following month. Rowe's play was not actually the "next" one, as it followed Vanbrugh's *The*

being all new Cloath'd, and Excellently well perform'd had a Successful run, but fell short of his *Ambitious Step-Mother*, and his *Tamerlane*.

Then was Acted a Comedy call'd the *Confederacy*,[362] wrote by Captain *Vantbrugg*, an Excellent Witty Play, and all Parts very well Acted: But the Nice *Criticks Censure* was, it wanted just *Decorum*; made it flag at last.

[49]

Trelooby a Farce, Wrote by Captain *Vantbrugg*: Mr. *Congreve* and Mr. *Walsh*.[363] Mr. *Dogget* Acting *Trelooby* so well, the whole was highly Applauded.

The Mistake,[364] Wrote by Captain *Vantbrugg*; a very diverting Comedy, Witty and good Humour in't, but will scarce be Enroll'd a Stock-Play.

Confederacy (next in Downes' list).

[362] Used to reopen the Haymarket, 30 October 1705. (Vanbrugh's company had returned to Lincoln's Inn Fields in late July "till Her Majesty's Theatre in the Hay-Market be intirely finish'd," as the company advertised in the *Daily Courant* on 19 July.) We have records of five, possibly six, performances in the first run.

[363] Originally acted at Lincoln's Inn Fields on 30 March 1704. Downes is evidently thinking of the Haymarket revival of 28 January 1706, "The last Act being entirely new." At that time we have record of six performances in the next fifteen acting days. This version was not printed, though an unacted translation-adaptation of the same material was published by John Ozell a few weeks after the performance. James Ralph printed *The Cornish Squire* in 1734 with the claim that it represented the work of Congreve, Vanbrugh, and Walsh—a claim that has been hotly debated by modern scholars. For a summary of the controversy, concluding that there is no evidence that any extant text gives the acted version of 1704, see Graham D. Harley, "*Squire Trelooby* and *The Cornish Squire*: A Reconsideration," *Philological Quarterly*, 49 (1970), 520-529.

[364] Premièred 27 December 1705. It ran six nights initially and added two more performances its first month.

The next new Play was, *The Revolution of Sweden;*[365] Wrote by Mrs. *Trotter*, she kept close to the History, but wanting the just Decorum of Plays, expir'd the Sixth Day.

Then a new Opera call'd, *The British Enchanters,*[366] Wrote by the Honourable Mr. *George Greenvil*; very Exquisitly done, especially the Singing Part; making Love the *Acme* of all Terrestrial Bliss: Which infinitely arrided both Sexes, and pleas'd the Town as well as any *English* Modern Opera.

After this was perform'd, an Opera, call'd *The Temple of Love;*[367] consisting all of Singing and Dancing: The Singing Compos'd by Monsieur *Sidgeon:*[368] The Version into *English*, by Monsieur *Moteux* from the *Italian*: The Singing perform'd by Mr. *Laurence*, Mr. *Laroon*, Mr. *Cook,*[369] Mrs. *Bracegirdle, Maria Gallia*, and several other Men and Women for the Chorus's: The Dances, made and perform'd all by *French* Men; it lasted but Six Days, and answer'd not their Expectation.

---

[365] Premièred 11 February 1706. We have record of only four performances, and the fullness of the calendar at this time makes more unlikely.

[366] First performed on 21 February 1706. A traditional semi-opera (music by Eccles and William Corbett), staged by Betterton. It was a considerable success, enjoying twelve performances during its first season. On the complex history of this work, see Stoddard Lincoln, "The Anglicization of *Amadis de Gaul*," *On Stage and Off*, ed. John W. Ehrstine, et al. (Pullman: Washington State Univ. Press, 1968), pp. 46-52.

[367] Premièred 7 March 1706. Newspaper ads suggest that it received only two performances, the second on 16 March.

[368] I.e., Guiseppe Fedelli (or Joseph Saggione, *fl.* 1680-1733), musician and husband of Maria Gallia.

[369] This is the first known role for Mr. Lawrence, a singer who performed regularly at the theatres and in the opera until 1717. "F. Laroon" (i.e., Marcellus Laroon) is otherwise recorded only at Drury Lane between December 1702 and February 1703 and at a York Buildings concert on 29 March 1704. See *Biographical Dictionary*, IX, 157-159. Mr. Cook was a minor singer intermittently active in the London theatres between ca. 1694 and 1718. See *Biographical Dictionary*, III, 442-443.

The last Opera was, *The Kingdom of Birds*;[370] made by Mr. *Durfey*, perform'd in *July*, 1706. The Singers in't were, Mr. *Cook*, Mr. *Laroon*, Mr. *Laurence*, Mrs. *Hudson* and others: Dancers were, Monsieur *De Bargues*,[371] Monsieur *L'Abbe*'s

[50]

Brother,[372] Mr. *Fairbank*,[373] Mrs. *Elford* and others: It lasted only Six Days, not answering half the Expences of it.

After this, Captain *Vantbrugg* gave leave to Mr. *Verbruggen* and Mr. *Booth*,[374] and all the Young Company,[375] to Act the remainder of the Summer, what Plays they cou'd by their Industry get up for their own Benefit; continuing till *Bartholomew-Eve*, 23d,

---

[370] Thomas Durfey's *The Wonders in the Sun; or The Kingdom of the Birds*, premièred 5 April 1706. Only five performances can be documented. *The London Stage* fails to record Downes' account of the singers and dancers.

[371] Mons. Desbarques performed in London between November 1705 and May 1708. Writing in 1712, John Weaver called him the best serious dancer who had ever performed in England (*Biographical Dictionary*, IV, 341).

[372] Virtually nothing else is known of him except that he danced at Lincoln's Inn Fields on 20 February 1705.

[373] Charles Fairbank (*d.* 1729), dancer and choreographer active with the company from 1702 to 1706 (*Biographical Dictionary*, V, 136-137).

[374] Barton Booth (ca. 1679-1733) joined the Lincoln's Inn Fields Company in 1700. His success as Cato in 1713 was to be his springboard to a part in the Triumvirate management of Drury Lane and a place as one of the leading tragic actors of the day, but at this time he was still a young hopeful, mostly confined to secondary roles.

[375] Exactly what Downes means we cannot be certain. Hirelings were traditionally allowed to act for their own benefit in the summer, but as far as we know all members of this company were salaried; there were no "sharers." Probably what Downes means is that those actors who needed the money—mostly younger ones—made up this summer company.

of *August*, 1706, ending on that Day, with *The London Cuckolds*:[376] But in all that time their Profit Amounted not to half their Salaries, they receiv'd in Winter.

From *Bartholomew* day 1706, to the 15*th*, of *October* following, there was no more *Acting* there.[377]

In this Interval Captain *Vantbrugg* by Agreement with Mr. *Swinny*,[378] and by the Concurrence of my Lord Chamberlain, Transferr'd and Invested his License and Government of the Theatre to Mr. *Swinny*; who brought with him from Mr. *Rich*,[379] Mr. *Wilks*, Mr. *Cyber*, Mr. *Mills*, Mr. *Johnson*, Mr. *Keene*, Mr. *Norris*, Mr.

---

[376] Confirmed by the *Daily Courant* ad of 23 August: "It being the last time of Acting till after Bartholomew Fair."

[377] A statement borne out by newspaper ads.

[378] On 14 August 1706 Vanbrugh agreed to rent the Haymarket theatre, stock, and license to Owen Swiney for a term of seven years at a rent of £5 per acting day. See P.R.O. LC 7/2, fol. 1. The agreement is printed as an interdocument in *Vice Chamberlain Coke's Theatrical Papers*, p. 7. Swiney joined the Drury Lane theatre by the season of 1702-03 and soon moved into management. He took over the opera license in April 1712, quickly went bankrupt, and fled to the Continent in January 1713. He spent many years in Italy as an agent for British patrons of such painters as Canaletto, Cimaroli, Piazzetta, and Pittoni. See Francis Haskell, *Patrons and Painters* (New York: Knopf, 1963), pp. 287-292. He returned to London in the 1730s (as Owen MacSwiney) and competed with his old friend Colley Cibber for the favours of Peg Woffington.

[379] Congreve describes this shuffle in a letter of 10 September 1706 to Joseph Keally: "The play-houses have undergone another revolution; and Swinny, with Wilks, Mrs Olfield [sic], Pinkethman, Bullock, and Dicky [Norris], are come over to the Hay-Market. Vanbrugh resigns his authority to Swinny .... My Lord Chamberlain approves and ratifies the desertion." *Congreve: Letters and Documents*, no. 26. Swiney's long letter to Cibber of 5 October explains the power politics and secret bargains involved in this reshuffle. The letter is preserved in holograph in the Osborn Collection, Yale University, and is published as an interdocument in *Vice Chamberlain Coke's Theatrical Papers*, pp. 11-13.

Fairbank, Mrs. *Oldfield*[380] and others; United them to the Old Company; Mr. *Betterton* and Mr. *Underhill*, being the only remains of the Duke of *York*'s Servants, from 1662, till the Union in *October* 1706.[381] Now having given an Account of all the Principal Actors and Plays, down to 1706. I with the said Union, conclude my History.

Next follows the Account of the present Young Company (which United with the Old, in *October, 1706*.)[382] Now Acting at the Theatre Royal in *Drury-Lane*; Her Majesty's Company of Comedians, under the Government of Col. *Brett*.[383]

---

[380] Anne Oldfield joined the Patent Company in 1699 and rapidly became the leading actress of her day.

[381] What Downes describes as a "Union" we now see as a temporary realignment preliminary to the genre division and complete union of the two acting companies ordered by the Lord Chamberlain on 31 December 1707 (P.R.O. LC 5/154, pp. 299-300; printed in *Vice Chamberlain Coke's Theatrical Papers*, pp. 49-50).

[382] The following survey provides capsule commentary on the principal performers who had been working for the Patent Company and hence were relatively unfamiliar to Downes. He probably started with Wilks, Cibber, and Estcourt because the three of them became (very temporarily, as it turned out) the managerial team at Drury Lane in March 1708. See the agreement transcribed in Fitzgerald, II, 443-446.

[383] Henry Brett (*d.* 1724) married Ann, former Countess of Macclesfield, in 1700, acquiring a large fortune in the process. He was Tory M.P. for Bishop's Castle, Salop., 1701-1708, and briefly held the rank of Lt. Col. in Sir Charles Hotham's regiment. Brett became one of the principal shareholders in the Patent Company as of 6 October 1707 when Sir Thomas Skipwith made him an outright gift of his share in the company (see Fitzgerald, I, 252-257). Brett took an active part in management throughout 1708, but when Skipwith decided in February 1709 that he wanted his share back, Brett yielded gracefully and disappeared from the theatrical scene. For the litigation involved in the return of the share, see P.R.O. C8/481/66 and C10/545/39 (transcribed by Hotson, pp. 386-397).

[51]

Mr. *Wilks*,[384] Proper and Comely in Person, of Graceful Port, Mein and Air; void of Affectation; his Elevations and Cadencies just, Congruent to Elocution: Especially in Gentile Comedy; not Inferior in Tragedy. The Emission of his Words free, easy and natural; Attracting attentive silence in his Audience, (I mean the Judicious) except where there are Unnatural Rants, As,

> --------------------------*I'le mount the Sky*,
> *And kick the G—ds like Foot-balls, as I fly:*

As Poet *D—rfy* has it,[385]

> *Which puts the Voice to such Obstreperous stretch,*
> *Requires the Lungs of a* Smith's *Bellows to reach.*

He is indeed the finisht Copy of his Famous Predecessor, Mr. *Charles Hart*.[386]

Mr. *Cyber*,[387] A Gentleman of his time has Arriv'd to an

---

[384] Robert Wilks (ca. 1665-1732), who became the leading actor of his day. He acted briefly with the United Company in the early 1690s, spent some time in Dublin, and returned for good in 1698-99. Like Cibber, he was a member of the Triumvirate management of Drury Lane from its inception in 1709.

[385] We have not found the source of this quotation.

[386] Davies objects that Wilks did not leave Dublin for London until about 1690 and so could not have seen Hart, who died in 1683, adding that "*Cibber* with more truth tells us that *Wilks*'s model was *Montford*" (Waldron, 1789, p. 67). But Downes' point seems to be that in his range and abilities Wilks was the kind of actor Hart had been.

[387] Colley Cibber (1671-1757) joined the United Company in 1690 but did not get major parts until the division of 1695. By 1708 his line in fops was well established, and Downes' comparison with Mountfort suggests genuine admiration. The roles for which he particularly commends Cibber are in Vanbrugh's *The Relapse*, Etherege's *The Man of Mode*, and Crowne's *Sir Courtly Nice*. As a member of the Triumvirate management at Drury

exceeding Perfection, in hitting justly the Humour of a starcht
Beau, or Fop; as the Lord *Fopington*; Sir *Fopling* and Sir *Courtly*,
equalling in the last, the late Eminent Mr. *Mounfort*, not much
Inferior in Tragedy, had Nature given him Lungs Strenuous to his
finisht Judgment.

Mr. *Escourt*,[388] *Histrio Natus*; he has the Honour (Nature
enduing him with an easy, free, unaffected Mode of Elocution) in
Comedy always to Lætificate his Audience, especially Quality, (Witness Serjeant *Kyte*). He's not Excellent only in that, but a Superlative Mimick.

[52]

Mr. *Booth*, A Gentleman of liberal Education, of form Venust;
of Mellifluent Pronuntiation, having proper Gesticulations, which
are Graceful Attendants of true Elocution; of his time a most Compleat Tragedian.[389]

Mr. *Johnson*,[390] He's Skilful in the Art of Painting, which is a

---

Lane, Cibber was one of the most powerful—and hated—figures in the London theatre from 1709 to his retirement from management in 1732. His
Apology (1740) remains one of the principal supplements to Downes on the
period 1690 to 1708.

[388] Richard Estcourt (1668-1712) came to London from Dublin in October 1704 and quickly became a popular attraction. He created the role of
Serjeant Kite in Farquhar's *The Recruiting Officer* (1706), for which he
was highly praised. (See, for example, Steele in the *Tatler* of 26 May
1709.) Estcourt was particularly successful as a mimic, apparently
endowed with a good voice and clear speech despite his Irish background.

[389] On Booth, see note 374, above. Booth's liberal education was
obtained at Westminster School. "Venust" means handsome by courtesy
of the goddess of Love. Booth was a Betterton protégé and therefore one of
the actors of whom Downes particularly approved.

[390] Benjamin Johnson (1665-1742) joined the Patent Company about
1695, so Downes did not know him well. Of the roles mentioned, Morose is
in *The Silent Woman*, Corbaccio in *Volpone*, Hothead in Crowne's *Sir
Courtly Nice*. Davies had high praise for Johnson from personal observa-
tion, saying that he was "a very correct and chaste Comedian. He was the

great Adjument, very Promovent to the Art of true Elocution, which
is always requirable in him, that bears the Name of an Actor;[391] he
has the Happiness to gain Applause from Court and City: Witness,
Morose, Corbaccio, Mr. *Hothead* and several others; He is a true
Copy of Mr. *Underhill*, whom Sir *William Davenant* judg'd 40 Year
ago in *Lincolns-Inn-Fields*, the truest Comedian in his Company.

Mr. *Dogget*.[392] On the Stage, he's very Aspectabund,[393] wearing a Farce in his Face; his Thoughts deliberately framing his
Utterance Congruous to his Looks: He is the only Comick Original
now Extant: Witness, *Ben, Solon, Nikin*, The *Jew* of *Venice*, &c.

Mr. *Pinkethman*, He's the darling of *Fortunatus*, he has gain'd
more in Theatres and Fairs in Twelve Years, than those that have
Tugg'd at the Oar of Acting these 50.[394]

---

most exact copy of Nature I ever saw. But he wanted that warmth of Col-
ouring which *Cibber* gave to his comic characters, and which Mr. *Garrick*
has since carried still higher. *Weston* was another *Johnson*" (Waldron,
1789, p. 68).

[391] Waldron says "I apprehend this means the painting of the face, and
marking it with dark lines to imitate the wrinkles of old age" (p. 68).
However W. R. Chetwood (the Triumvirate's sometime prompter) says that
Johnson trained as a painter. See *A General History of the Stage* (London:
W. Owen, 1749), p. 174.

[392] Thomas Doggett (ca. 1670?-1721), though enormously popular as a
comic actor, was in and out of London in the early years of the century
because he could not get along with managers. When Downes wrote, Doggett had not been active in London since 1705-06, but he did six guest
appearances at the Haymarket in March 1708. Briefly a Triumvir with
Wilks and Cibber from 1709, he walked out at the time of Booth's enforced
admission to management in 1713. Of the roles mentioned, Ben is the
sailor in Congreve's *Love for Love*; Solon is in Durfey's *The Marriage-Hater
Match'd*; Nikin is the pet name of Fondlewife in Congreve's *The Old Batchelour*; the Jew of Venice is in Granville's 1701 adaptation of *The Mer-
chant of Venice*.

[393] This coinage seems to mean that Doggett acted with his face more
than was usual.

[394] A Patent Company comedian, William Pinkethman (*d.* 1725) spe-
cialized in gags and low comedy routines. As a fair and summer theatre

Next Mr. *Mills*,[395] Mr. *Powel*,[396] Mr. *Bullock*;[397] the 2 first Excell in Tragedy; the other in Comedy, &c.

I must not Omit Praises due to *Mr. Betterton*, The first and now only remain of the old Stock, of the Company of Sir *William Davenant* in *Lincolns-Inn-Fields*; he like an old Stately Spreading Oak now stands fixt, Environ'd round with brave Young Growing, Flourishing Plants: There needs nothing to speak his Fame, more than the following Parts.[398]

---

manager he was a brilliant publicist and skilful entrepreneur.

[395] John Mills (*d.* 1736) was a Patent Company actor who joined in 1695, a friend of Wilks' promoted into better roles over Booth's head.

[396] George Powell (ca. 1668?-1714), son of the King's Company actor Martin Powell, grew up in the theatre but never fulfilled his promise. He felt that Betterton kept him down, but by the time he became deputy manager for Rich in 1695 he had a serious drinking problem, and the more reliable Wilks soon replaced him. Despite Powell's undoubted ability as a performer, he bounced back and forth between the two theatres in the following decade.

[397] William Bullock, Senior (ca. 1667-1742) joined the Patent Company in 1695, so Downes did not know him well. Sir Tunbelly Clumsey in *The Relapse* and Boniface in *The Beaux Stratagem* were typical of his roles.

[398] See Judith Milhous, "An Annotated Census of Thomas Betterton's Roles, 1659-1710," *Theatre Notebook*, 29 (1975), 33-43, 85-94; and Bruce Podewell, *ibid*, 32 (1978), 89-90. We can document more than 180 certain roles for Betterton, and given the incompleteness of our performance records, we may assume that the actual total is significantly higher. Students of Betterton's roles should note that Gildon's "Catalogue of Plays in which Mr. *Betterton* made some considerable Figure" in his 1710 *Life of Betterton*, pp. 174-175, is almost certainly derived from Downes. Gildon's list begins from page 18 of the 1708 edition of *Roscius Anglicanus* and continues with plays in the exact order Downes gives them (with some omissions) through page 46, where instead of *Merry Wives* Gildon inserts "Harry *the IVth*." He then skips to *The British Enchanters* on p. 49. We conclude that Gildon's list has virtually no independent authority, especially not before the 1690s.

Pericles Prince of *Tyre.*	*Solyman* the Magnificent.[399]
The Bondman.	*Hamlet.*
Ca'sar Borgia.	*Macbeth.*
The Loyal Subject.	*Timon* of *Athens.*
The Mad Lover.	*Othello.*
Richard the Third.	*Oedipus.*
King *Lear.*	*Jaffeir.*
	King *Henry* the Eighth.
	Sir John *Falstaff.*

Mr. *Dryden* a little before his Death in a Prologue, rendring him this PRAISE.

> *He like the setting Sun, still shoots a Glimmery Ray,*
> *Like Antient* ROME *Majestick in decay.*[400]

FINIS.

----

[399] Betterton played characters of this name in both Davenant's *The Siege of Rhodes* and Orrery's *Mustapha.*

[400] Summers (p. 282) points out that these lines occur not in a prologue but in Dryden's complimentary poem prefixed to Granville's *Heroick Love* (pub. 1698). The lines actually read:
> Their Setting Sun still shoots a Glim'ring Ray,
> Like Ancient *Rome*, Majestick in Decay.

Endnotes

Endnote 1: List of the "Old Stock Plays" (pages 24-25)

Jonson's *Catiline's Conspiracy* (1611) was rumoured to be in rehearsal at Bridges Street on 11 December 1667.

Shakespeare's *The Merry Wives of Windsor* (ca. 1597-1602) was included in a list of plays acted at the Red Bull in the summer and early autumn of 1660 (see *The Dramatic Records of Sir Henry Herbert*, p. 82); it was performed at Vere Street on 9 November 1660.

Shirley's *The Opportunity* (1634) was played by 26 November 1660.

Shirley's *The Example* (1634) is unrecorded in the Carolean period except by Downes.

Brome's *The Jovial Crew* (1641) was played by 25 July 1661.

Beaumont and Fletcher's *Philaster* (ca. 1608-1610) was played at the Red Bull in the summer and early autumn of 1660 and at Vere Street on 13 November.

Shirley's *The Cardinal* (1641) was definitely performed by 23 July 1662.

Jonson's *Bartholomew Fair* (1614) was first revived on 8 June 1661.

Fletcher's *The Chances* (ca. 1613-1625) was played by 24 November 1660; a revision by Buckingham may have been performed in 1664 and was definitely on stage by February 1667.

Middleton's *The Widow* (ca. 1615-1617) was played by the Red Bull company in the summer and early autumn of 1660, at Vere Street on 16 November.

Jonson's *The Devil is an Ass* (1616) was referred to in the prologue to *The Cheats* as if it were in the repertory about March 1663, but no more specific evidence for it is known.

Glapthorne's *Argulus and Parthenia* (ca. 1632-1638) was first revived on 31 January 1661.

Jonson's *Every Man in His Humour* (1598) was probably played before Easter 1670, his *Every Man Out* (1599) by July 1675.

Thomas Porter's *The Carnival*, a new play, received its première ca. autumn 1663.

Jonson's *Sejanus* (1603) is undocumented in the Carolean period except by Downes. Rights to it were assigned to the King's Company in

January 1669 (P.R.O. LC 5/12, pp. 212-213).

Dekker's (?) *The Merry Devil of Edmonton* (ca. 1599-1604) was played by 10 August 1661.

Webster's *The White Devil* ("Vittoria Corumbona," ca. 1609-1612) was performed by 2 October 1661.

Fletcher and Massinger's *The Beggars' Bush* (ca. 1615-1622) was played by the Red Bull company on 7 November 1660, by the Vere Street company on 20 November.

Shirley's *The Traitor* (1631) was given by the Red Bull company on 6 November 1660, at Vere Street on 22 November.

Shakespeare's *Titus Andronicus* (1594) is undocumented before its 1678 alteration except by Downes.

Endnote 2:   The cast for *Sophonisba* (pages 39-40)

Differences between this cast and those in the quartos of 1676 and 1681 suggest that Downes' cast is derived from a revival ca. 1677-78 rather than from the original production. For Mohun, Kynaston, Hart, and Clark, Q1676 gives the same roles as Downes and Q1681, but on some other roles it differs from either. Q1676 gives: Maherbal—Wats[on?]; Bomilcar—Haris; Lelius—Wintersel; Sophonisba—Mrs. Cosh; Rosalinda—Mrs. Damport. In their edition of Lee, Thomas B. Stroup and Arthur L. Cooke point out that besides naming a character who never appears, Q1676 shows stop-press corrections, including extensive additions. They suggest that it "was hurriedly composed by someone at the printer's office who was not familiar either with the play itself or with the actors and actresses of the playhouse." See *The Works of Nathaniel Lee*, 2 vols. (1954-55; rpt. Metuchen, N.J.: Scarecrow, 1968), I, 79-84. Nevertheless, Q1676 could represent the original cast if we assume that Burt was sick or otherwise temporarily unavailable in April 1675. If so, then when he returned and took over Maherbal, Watson was demoted to Varro, as in Q1681. William Harris had left the company by 1677-78, so Wintershall moved up to Bomilcar, leaving Lelius for Lydall, as Downes and Q1681 agree. Edward Lydall disappears from the records after the summer of 1677, but he was a minor performer who might have acted another season or two without getting his name in a cast list. Q1681 also adds: Trebellius—Powell; Menander—Griffin.

The female roles offer different problems. The "Mrs. Cosh" of Q1676 is probably a deformation of "Mrs. Cox," on whom Downes and Q1681 agree for Sophonisba. (The name might refer to Mrs. Coysh, a stroller whose husband worked at least irregularly with the King's Company from 1672 to 1679, but she is not known to have performed in London and is not plausible in the title role.) "Damport" is a common deformation of Elizabeth Bowtell's maiden name, Davenport. However odd its application to her some six years after her marriage, that seems likelier than the importation of an otherwise unknown actress into a role Bowtell was occupying shortly thereafter. Q1681 also names Mrs. Nep as Aglave and Mrs. Corey as Cumana, Priestesses of Bellona. We cannot agree with Stroup and Cooke that Q1681 represents the Oxford production of 1681 because Bowtell, Burt, and Knepp were not active at that time, and Wintershall died in July 1679. We conclude that both Downes and Q1676 are trustworthy, the peculiarities of the quarto cast notwithstanding. Q1681 seems to represent the same revival Downes records.

Endnote 3:   When did Rhodes' Company begin to perform?
             (page 43)

Monck's troops entered England on 2 January 1660 and arrived in London on 3 February. Thus Downes probably means that Rhodes commenced operations ca. February 1659/60. Rhodes had held the lease on the Cockpit since 1649, and Lilleston (one of his actors) was arrested for an unlawful performance at the Cockpit on 4 February 1659/60 (Hotson, pp. 99, 197). Whether Rhodes ever got "a License from the then Governing State" is questionable. Both Bulstrode Whitelock (*Memorials of English Affairs*, 1732, p. 699) and "The Diurnal of Thomas Rugg" (British Library Add. MS 10,116, p. 128) note an "Order of the Council forbidding stage-players to act" (23 April 1660), and no record of a license from Herbert survives. On 28 July 1660 Rhodes paid a fee of £4 6s to parish authorities for the right to act. The fee was stated to be 2d per day, but Hotson shows that this is an error for 2s—i.e., 43 performances. (See John Parton, *Some Account of the Hospital and Parish of St. Giles in the Fields, Middlesex* [London: Luke Hansard, 1822], p. 236; and Hotson, p. 198.) On 18 August 1660 Pepys attended a play at the Cockpit, evidently performed by Rhodes' troupe. Thus Rhodes' operations in London seem to fall between early February and late August 1660, when Davenant and Killigrew obtained their monopoly (British Library Add. MS 19,256, fol. 47, dated

21 August). After that time Rhodes probably became a sub-manager for Davenant: he is named as receiver of payment for a Duke's Company performance of *Ignoramus*, 1 November 1662 (P.R.O. LC 5/138, p. 91, dated 17 October 1663). On 2 January 1663/4 Rhodes received a strollers' license, valid during pleasure, for performance throughout Charles' realms, London and Westminster excepted (P.R.O. LC 5/138, p. 387).

Endnote 4:   Plays performed from 1662 to 1665 (page 59)

No performance dates are known for Middleton's *A Trick to Catch the Old One* (ca. 1604-1607) or Brome's *The Sparagus Garden* (1635). Pepys saw Glapthorne's *Wit in a Constable* (ca. 1636-1638) on 23 May 1662, the first day it was revived. The Red Bull Company gave Cooke's *Greene's Tu Quoque* (1611) in Oxford on 3 July 1661; the only recorded performance by the Duke's Company occurred 12 September 1667, with alterations by Davenant. On Shakespeare's *Lear*, see note 167, above. Stapylton's *The Slighted Maid* was seen by Pepys on 23 February 1663, probably in its first run. Dr. Edward Browne saw *The Step-Mother* about October 1663 (close to the première): see Robert D. Hume, "Dr. Edward Browne's Playlists." Davenant's *The Law Against Lovers*, a conflation of *Measure for Measure* and *Much Ado*, was seen by foreign visitors on 15 February 1662, probably in its first run. On *'Tis Better* and *Worse and Worse*, see "Lost English Plays," nos. 12 and 13; to judge from the titles, these plays are probably translations of Calderón's *Mejor está que estaba* and *Peor está que estaba*. Downes is our only source on *'Tis Better*; Pepys saw *Worse and Worse* on 20 July 1664. He saw *The Ghosts* on 17 April 1665 (see "Lost English Plays," no. 20). No performance of *Pandora* is known. *The London Stage* assigns it to April 1664 because it was published in May, but from publication norms at the time, a production in 1662 or 1663 is much more likely.

Endnote 5:   Performers who left the Duke's Company by
              circa 1673 (page 74)

Joseph Price (*fl.* 1661-1664) is not definitely known to have acted in London after 1664; our only later record of him is in the highly problematical cast printed in the 1678 edition of *The Duchess of Malfi*. He may have moved to Dublin.

Thomas Lovell (*fl.* 1635-1663) is not recorded after 1663.

Thomas Lilleston is not definitely recorded after his appearance in Orrery's *King Henry the Fifth* in 1664.

The date of Robert Nokes' departure is uncertain. The cast given for Orrery's *King Henry the Fifth* (1664) in Bodleian MS Rawl. Poet 2 implies that he took the part of the Duke of Exeter at that time—his last recorded role.

We have no record of John Moseley after women replaced boys in female roles ca. 1661.

John "Cogaine" was sworn a comedian on 24 February 1665 (P.R.O. LC 3/25, p. 162). Downes' report is our only means of dating his death.

Mr. Floyd is not definitely recorded after 1664, except in the problematical cast in the 1676 edition of *Hamlet*. Downes' comment is our only indication of a death date.

Mr. Gibbons is known only from this report of his demise.

Hester Davenport withdrew from the stage by February 1662, though she may have returned to perform in *The Adventures of Five Hours* in January 1663. Downes' assertion that she acted in *Mustapha* in 1665 is almost certainly an error; see p. 58, above.

Mary Davis retired from the public theatre in 1668, though she appeared in *Calisto* and perhaps in other court entertainments in the 1670s.

Mrs. Jennings can be documented from November 1662 through the spring of 1671, but not after that. *The London Stage Index* implies that she performed Mercury in *Calisto* in 1675, but that part was played by Sarah Jennings, later Churchill, the future Duchess of Marlborough.

Endnote 6:   Performers who joined the Duke's Company circa
              1673 (pages 74-75)

Anthony Leigh probably joined in spring or summer 1672. In December 1671 the Lord Chamberlain ordered Leigh and four other actors arrested for performing without a license. See P.R.O. LC 5/14, p. 96 (reversed). His first known role with a patent company is Pacheco in *The Reformation* (spring or summer 1672?). *The London Stage* lists him in the Duke's Company for the season of 1671-72, but does so on the basis of an implausible 1671 date for *Herod and Mariamne*, evidently performed ca. August 1673.

Thomas Gillow's first known role was in *Herod and Mariamne* (ca. August 1673?). He was acting regularly with the company by 1674-75.

Thomas Jevon (1652-1688) became a celebrated low comedian. His first recorded activity with the Duke's Company is Downes' anecdote about him rehearsing in Settle's *The Conquest of China* in May 1675 (see page 75, above). By 1676 he is named regularly in company casts.

Thomas Percival was definitely with the company by November 1674 when he performed in Settle's *Love and Revenge*. If the problematical cast in the 1678 edition of *The Duchess of Malfi* is accurate, he was with the company before Cademan was disabled in August 1673. *The London Stage* lists him in the 1671-72 roster, but does so on the basis of a speculative assignment of the 1678 *Duchess* cast to a performance on 31 January 1672. Thomas Percival is best remembered as the father of Susanna Percival Mountfort Verbruggen. He seems to have been squeezed out of the United Company in the mid-eighties and died in 1693 while awaiting transportation for clipping coins.

In 1691 Joseph Williams described himself as "about 28," so he was born about 1663 (P.R.O. C24/1144, deposition 55). Lack of birth dates has led to confusion of his roles with those of David Williams, who was active between 1675 and 1682. According to the *Biographical Dictionary* entry (forthcoming), the first time Joseph was distinguished from David in print was in the 1679 quarto of *The Destruction of Troy*, where he is listed for Troilus. He created Polydore in *The Orphan* at only 18, and he was a sharing actor in the United Company by 1691. His inclusion in the *London Stage* roster for 1662-63 is an error; a different Williams must have performed in *Ignoramus* on 1 November 1662.

John Boman's probable dates are ca. 1651?-1739. His first recorded appearance was in Behn's *The Counterfeit Bridegroom* (spring 1677?), but if he joined as a "Boy" he probably started his training ca. 1670 or earlier, especially if he was born in 1651. Curll gives 1664 as his birthdate, but this seems too late, given his known roles in the seventies.

Elizabeth Barry was unquestionably the most important actress of her time. Her first recorded appearance was as Draxilla in *Alcibiades* (October 1675).

Elizabeth Currer's first definite role was in *The Conquest of China* (May 1675).

Charlotte Butler apparently performed in *Calisto* in 1675, but her first recorded appearances with the Duke's Company are in *Fools Have*

Fortune and *The Orphan* in January and February 1680. For the former, see Judith Milhous and Robert D. Hume, "The Prologue and Epilogue for *Fools Have Fortune, or Luck's All*," *Huntington Library Quarterly*, 43 (1980), 313-321.

Mrs. Slaughter's only known role under that name was Cornelia in Crowne's *The History of Charles VIII* (November 1671). Most modern authorities have accepted Genest's deduction (I, 156) that she became Mrs. Margaret Osborne by marriage in 1672. Mrs. Osborne played small parts with the Duke's and United Companies from 1672 to 1691. She appears in a roster of the Lincoln's Inn Fields actors as late as 20 July 1695 (Kent Archives Office, U269 F8/1).

Mrs. Knapper's only known roles fall between *Tom Essence* (ca. August 1676) and *A Fond Husband* (May 1677).

Mrs. Twyford's first known role was Emilia in *The Man of Mode* (March 1676)—if we assume that Downes' cast represents the first production. Her only other recorded role prior to 1682 was in *Circe* (May 1677), for which Downes is again our only authority. She played secondary roles in the United Company from 1682 through at least 1685-86. We suspect that she was intermittently absent for childbearing or amatory reasons early in her career.

Endnote 7:   Plays revived by the United Company circa 1682-1685
(page 83)

Fletcher's *The Scornful Lady* was performed before Charles II on 23 February 1684.

Wycherley's *The Plain-Dealer* was performed at the Inner Temple on 1 November 1683. Edward A. Langhans ("New Restoration Manuscript Casts," *Theatre Notebook*, 27 [1973], 152-153) reports a probable cast for the United Company period: Manly—Betterton (?); Vernish—Griffin (?); Oldfox—Anthony Leigh; Plausible—Mountfort; Blackacre—James Nokes. (Fidelia and Olivia are omitted.)

Dryden's *The Mock Astrologer* (i.e., *An Evening's Love*) was performed at court on 16 February 1686.

Brome's *The Jovial Crew* was probably produced by the United Company in the autumn of 1683, to judge by the cast in the edition advertised in the *Term Catalogues* in February 1684.

Fletcher's *The Beggars' Bush* was performed before James II on 1

December 1686.

Jonson's *Bartholomew Fair* is not definitely recorded in the decade after the union, but we have no reason to doubt Downes' assertion that the United Company revived the play. Downes' comment about James Nokes replacing Wintershall in the role of Cokes (page 42, above) strongly implies a United Company revival before Nokes' retirement ca. 1691.

Shakespeare's *The Moor of Venice* (i.e., *Othello*) was performed before Charles II on 18 January 1683.

Fletcher's *Rollo, or the Bloody Brother* was performed before the Queen on 20 January 1685.

Fletcher's *The Humorous Lieutenant* was seen by Charles II on 2 January 1685.

Fletcher's *The Double Marriage* was seen by James II on 6 February 1688.

Endnote 8:   The best singers and dancers (page 98)

Mary Lindsey had joined Drury Lane by the time of *The World in the Moon* (late June 1697) and continued to be a popular if temperamental performer until about 1710, after which Italian singers crowded her out of the opera.

Mrs. Hodgson was one of the most popular theatre singers from 1690 to 1706 (*Biographical Dictionary*, VII, 354-355).

Richard Leveridge, actor, singer, and composer, joined the Patent Company in 1695 and remained a popular performer for decades. He is tentatively set down for an annual salary of £40 as the "Master to teach" singers in the "Company Plan" of 1703 (P.R.O. LC 7/3, fols. 161-164). On this document, see Judith Milhous, "The Date and Import of the Financial Plan for a United Theatre Company in P.R.O. LC 7/3," *Maske und Kothurn*, 21 (1975), 81-88.

Philippe du Ruel first appeared at Drury Lane in January 1703, serving as the Patent Company's answer to L'Abbé. In the "Company Plan" of 1703 his hypothetical salary for a year is £40. He left London after the season of 1706-07.

René Cherrier was a popular dancer and choreographer active in London from December 1703 to May 1708 (*Biographical Dictionary*, III, 189-190).

Mrs. Elford was a dancer active in London ca. 1700-1706. See

Biographical Dictionary, V, 47. She is tentatively set down for an annual salary of £40 in the "Company Plan" of 1703.

Mary Anne Campion (ca. 1687-1706) joined the Drury Lane company in 1698 as a child singer and retired to become the mistress of the Duke of Devonshire ca. March 1704. She was a highly successful singer and dancer (*Biographical Dictionary*, III, 31-32). Whether Miss Campion took part in this command performance seems very doubtful; Downes is evidently using the occasion to give a list of adjunct performers.

Du Ruel's wife, Eleanor, danced at Drury Lane from the spring of 1704 through the spring of 1706. The Du Ruels' first names are given in a letter quoted in Winston S. Churchill, *Marlborough: His Life and Times*, 2 vols. (London: Harrap, 1933-34), I, 926.

The "Devonshire Girl" (i.e., Mrs. Mosse), a popular dancer, performed at Drury Lane from the autumn of 1702 through the spring of 1706.

Appendix

Key Dates and Events

1660   Charles II authorizes patents for two theatre companies.

        The King's Company, largely composed of the personnel who had
        been active at the Red Bull, commences operations at the Vere
        Street theatre with Thomas Killigrew as patentee.

        The Duke's Company, under the leadership of its patentee, Sir
        William Davenant, absorbs Rhodes' Company, consisting largely
        of beginners. The company opens at Salisbury Court.

1661   The Duke's Company opens its new Lincoln's Inn Fields theatre,
        equipped with changeable scenery.

1663   The King's Company, stung by competition, opens a changeable-
        scenery theatre of its own in Bridges Street.

1665   The theatres are closed for eighteen months by plague.

1668   Davenant dies, and legal control of the Duke's Company passes
        to his widow, acting for their son Charles, a minor. Senior
        actors Henry Harris and Thomas Betterton assume manage-
        ment of the company.

1671   The Duke's Company triumphantly opens its fancy new theatre
        in Dorset Garden.

1672   The Bridges Street theatre is destroyed by fire. The King's Com-
        pany moves temporarily to the Lincoln's Inn Fields theatre, just
        vacated by its rivals.

1674   The King's Company opens its new Drury Lane theatre.

1677   Charles Killigrew wins legal control of the King's Company in
        litigation with his father.

1678   About this time Henry Harris retires from acting and is replaced by William Smith as co-manager of the Duke's Company.

1682   Union of the two companies. In essence, the Duke's Company absorbs the sickly King's Company, though the joint troupe uses both Drury Lane and Dorset Garden.

1687   Charles Davenant sells his interest in the United Company to his brother, Alexander. Thomas Davenant becomes manager, but the company continues to rely on Betterton's managerial advice.

1693   Alexander Davenant flees his creditors and absconds to the Canary Islands. Sir Thomas Skipwith and Christopher Rich, from whom Davenant had borrowed the money to buy into the theatre, take control of the company.

1694   Betterton and other senior actors rebel against the Skipwith-Rich management.

1695   Lord Chamberlain Dorset sides with the rebel actors and grants them a license to act during the King's pleasure. The rebels remodel the Lincoln's Inn Fields theatre and set up a cooperative company there. Skipwith and Rich rebuild their troupe (now directed by George Powell) and continue to occupy Drury Lane and Dorset Garden.

1704   Vanbrugh and Congreve receive a license and take over direction of the Lincoln's Inn Fields company.

1705   Vanbrugh opens his elegant new theatre in the Haymarket.

1706   Congreve drops out of the management; Vanbrugh assigns his license and theatre to Owen Swiney, a former deputy of Rich's at Drury Lane. Swiney engineers a major reorganization and steals several of Rich's principal performers. In this reshuffle, the Haymarket's elderly prompter, John Downes, is forced into retirement and finds himself at leisure to write *Roscius Anglicanus*.

Textual Notes

All emendations other than the silent alterations covered in the explanation of textual policy are recorded here. The reading in the present edition is printed first, followed by the reading in the edition of 1708.

Page 4, line 2: continu'd] continu d

Page 9, line 3: Mrs. *Reeves*] Mrs. *Knight* (1708 errata as emended by Joseph Knight)

Page 11, line 1: Mrs. *Marshal*] Mr. *Marshal*

Page 14, line 7: Epicure Mammon] Ep. Mammon

Page 17, line 9: IX] X

Page 18, line 9: X] XI

Page 19, line 8: XI] XII

Page 21, line 3: XII] XIII

Page 21, line 10: XIII] XIV

Page 22 line 6: Mrs. *Knep*] Mr. *Knep*

Page 22, line 9: XIV] XV

Page 26 line 8: *Cidaria*] *Ciduria* (1708 errata)

Page 29, line 9: *Morat*] *Moral*

Page 31, line 6: *Eunuch*] *Enuch*

Page 32, line 7: Mrs. *Reeves*] Mr. *Reeves* (Q1673 of Dryden's play)

Page 33, line 9: *Aquilius*] *Aquitius* (1708 errata)

Page 34, line 7: *Daughter to*] *D. to*

Page 36, line 3: *Earl of* Southampton] *E. of* Southampton

Page 38, line 8: *King of* Spain] *K. of* Spain

Page 38, lines 11-12: *Queen of* Granada,] *Q. of* Gran.

Page 39, line 4: *Queen of* Spain] *Q. of* Spain

Page 39, line 9: Scipio] Scinio

Page 40, line 2: Rosalinda] Rosalnida

Page 40, line 6: *James's-Park*] *Jame's-Park*

Page 46, lines 9-10: *Wallingford*).] *Wallingford*)

Page 47, line 4: four following] three following (1708 errata)

Page 51, line 12: *Underhill*;] *Underhill*

Page 51, line 16: *Shakespear*] *Shaksepeur*

Page 52, line 4: *Medburn*);] *Medburn*)

Page 54, line 15: *Beaupre*] *Beanpre* (Q1663)

Page 54, line 15: *Boutefeu*] Bontefeu (Q1663)

Page 54, line 16: *Young. Maligni*] (Divided by an unnecessary paragraph break in the 1708 edition.)

Page 54, line 16: the Villain, Mr. *Saunford*; *Coligni*,] the Villain; Mr. *Saun-ford, Coligni*;

Page 54, line 18: part);] part)

Page 54, line 19: last.] last,

Page 55, line 5: Town.] Town

Page 55, line 8: Songs.] Songs

Page 56, line 5: Norfolk] Norfork

Page 57, line 7: *Sandford*;] *Sandford*,

Page 57, line 7: *Dacres*] *Daeres*

Page 57, line 8: *Will*,] *Will*.

Page 58, lines 10-11: Cardinal of *Veradium*] (Omitted in 1708 edition; supplied from the Dramatis Personae in the 1668 edition of Orrery's play.)

Page 58, line 11: *Young*:] *Young*.

Page 58, line 13: *Wiseman*):] *Wiseman*)

Page 61, line 12: *Charles's*] *Charle's*

Page 62, line 2: *Anthony. Gusman*] *Anthony Gusman*

Page 62, line 9: *Moleire*] *Moleiro* (1708 errata)

Page 64, line 6: together. When] together, when

Page 65, line 10: *Cuningham*] *Cunnigham*

Page 66, line 1: *Appius and Virginia*] *Appius Virginia*

Page 68, line 4: Mrs. *Leigh* Wife of Mr. *Antony Leigh*] Mrs. *Leigh* Wife, Mr. *John Lee* (1708 errata)

Page 68, line 9: *Davenant* her] *Davenant*) her

Page 69, line 10: House);] House)

Page 70, line 1: Sir *Symon Softhead*] Sir *Simeon Loft-head* (1708 errata)

Page 70, line 3: looked upon] look upon

Page 72, line 10: Poets.] Poets

Page 72, line 13: greater, *The Tempest*.] greater. *The Tempest*,

Page 73, line 6: Theatre);] Theatre)

Page 74, line 5: all things] all was things (1708 errata)

Page 75, line 4: *Tartars*] *Turtars*

Page 75, line 12: Double.] Double

Page 77, line 3: *Barry*:] *Barry*,

Page 77, line 3: *Betterton*:] *Betterton*,

Page 77, line 4: *Leigh*:] *Leigh*,

Page 78, lines 9-10: Reputation.] Reputation

Page 78, line 14: last.] last

Page 81, line 8: *Killigrew's*] *Killsgrew's*

Page 82, line 5: *Actors*.] *Actors*

Page 84, line 6: *Albanius*] *Albianus*

Page 85, line 4: *Surly,*] *Surly.*

Page 86, line 5: *Fumble.*] *Fumble*

Page 86, line 6: Fryar,] Fryar

Page 87, line 1: *Love*] *Lone*

Page 87, line 4: Acted in these Plays] Acted in this Play

Page 89, line 17: perform'd,] perform',d

Page 92, line 13: *Dilke*] *Dilks*

Page 93, line 8: *Love's*] *Lov's*

Page 95, line 6: answer'd] answer d

Page 95, line 6: expectation.] expectation

Page 97, line 6: *James's*] *Jame's*

Page 98, line 9: *Caius*] *Cains*

Page 101, line 7: last.] last

Page 101, line 9: *Walsh.*] *Walsh,*

Page 102, line 15: *French* Men] *French-*/Men

Page 104, line 4: *October*] *Octob.*

Page 107, line 9: *Kyte).*] *Kyte)*

Page 107, lines 11ff. (Page 52 in the edition of 1708 is set in smaller type than the rest of the text in order to conclude the book on E2v.)

Page 108, line 10: *Ben,*] *Ben.*

INDEX